THE COMPLETE GUIDE TO PAPILLONS

Tarah Schwartz

LP Media Inc. Publishing

Text copyright © 2019 by LP Media Inc.

Publication Data

Tarah Schwartz

The Complete Guide to Papillons ---- First edition.

Summary: "Successfully raising a Papillon dog from puppy to old age" --- Provided by publisher.

ISBN: 978-1-09498-611-1

[1. Papillons --- Non-Fiction] I. Title.

Design by Sorin Rădulescu

First paperback edition, 2019

TABLE OF CONTENTS

CHAPTER 1
The Papillon

What is a Papillon?

Papillons are a toy breed sometimes called the "Butterfly Dog" because of their large, fringed ears that resemble the wings of a butterfly. The Papillon is one the oldest toy breeds, having been depicted in Italian paintings in the 15th century. However, the breed hasn't always had the upright ears that it's known for today. Originally, this petite spaniel had drop ears, a variety known today as the Phalène. The breed was known as Continental Toy Spaniels at the time and the dogs were often painted alongside French and Italian royalty.

Papillons are active, affectionate dogs, retaining their puppy-like playfulness well into adulthood. They are confident, friendly dogs who tend to forget how small they are. They are not yappy dogs but will let you know when a visitor arrives. They generally prefer the companionship of humans over other animals and will gladly accompany you everywhere you go.

Photo Courtesy of
Kelsey Corn

Photo Courtesy of Tom Barcik

Although Papillons are known for their long, flowing coats, their silky hair is relatively easy to care for. They don't have the doggy odor common in other breeds and are not prone to matting. The breed does not have a double coat, so they don't experience heavy seasonal shedding. Papillons are a very clean breed and generally enjoy the grooming process. They are a "bath and brush" breed and do not require regular haircuts. Some owners may opt to trim around their paws and paw pads for a tidier appearance, but with regular brushing, the rest of their coat will look good year-round.

Although Papillons are not a common breed, they are by no means rare. The American Kennel Club (AKC) ranks them number 53 in popularity out of 193 breeds. The breed's popularity is growing, however, due to their lively, outgoing personalities and high activity levels. Handlers at dog shows claim they practically show themselves, prancing around the ring under the judge's eye. They are also an intelligent and easy-to-train breed, making them popular with competitors in agility and obedience. Papillon owners have also found success in tracking and barn hunt competitions.

Papillons are a relatively healthy breed, with few common genetic disorders. Although no breed can claim to be free from genetic problems, the Papillon is a very healthy breed compared to some. According to the Papillon Club of America, Papillons have an average lifespan of 11.45 years, but can live as long as 17 years.

History of the Papillon

The earliest representations of Papillons, known at the time as Continental Toy Spaniels, can be found in Italian paintings dating to the 1500s. Painters such as Tiziano Vicelli, Gonzales Coques, and Paolo Veronese included them in their work. A Papillon is even featured in a portrait of Louis XIV. The earlier depictions resemble today's drop-eared Phalène, as the erect ears of the breed did not become popular until later in the 19th century.

The popularity of the Continental Toy Spaniel among Europe's royalty led breeders to refine the signature characteristics of the breed. The dogs became finer-boned with a longer, more abundant coat. The skull became rounder and more distinguished from other types of spaniels. By the time of Louis XIV, Belgian and French breeders had achieved the look they desired.

In the earliest depictions, the ears of the Continental Toys Spaniel are of the drop variety and of medium size. They are set high on the skull, but far enough apart to see the round shape of the head. However, two paintings in the 18th century depict dogs with erect ears, suggesting that some Continental Toy Spaniels had ear leathers thick enough to stand up. Toward the end of the 19th century, more of these erect-eared dogs appeared, and the butterfly wing appearance became highly sought-after. Soon, the name Papillon became a popular term for the breed. The drop-eared variety was later called Phalène, French for "moth," because of the resemblance to the way moths carry their wings close to their bodies.

The Papillon was recognized by the AKC in 1935, when the Papillon Club of America was formed. However, the club was disbanded during the war and was not reformed until 1948. The first Papillon specialty show was held in September 1954 and the breed has been thriving since. In 1999, Ch. Loteki Supernatural Being, also known as Kirby, became the first Papillon to win Best in Show at the prestigious Westminster Kennel Club dog show. Today, the breed is a popular choice with competitors in all major dog sports. Papillons can be seen competing in conformation, obedience, agility, barn hunt, and even herding.

Physical Characteristics

Papillons are a dainty breed with an average height of 8"-12" at the shoulder. According to the breed standard, dogs over 11" will be faulted in the show ring, while dogs over 12" will be disqualified. Papillons typically weigh three to nine pounds. They are fine-boned, and their weight is in proportion to their height. Their bodies are slightly longer than their height measured at the withers.

The breed standard describes the Papillon's head as small and round with a fine, tapered muzzle. The skull must be slightly rounded between the ears. The ears, whether erect or drop, must be large and rounded at the tip. Papillons competing in conformation will be faulted for small, pointed ears, or ears that are set too high. They will also be penalized if both ears are not completely erect or completely drop. The teeth must meet in a scissor bite and the tongue must not be visible when the dog's jaws are closed. The neck is of medium length and the back is straight and level. The chest is of medium depth and the belly is tucked up. The tail is long, set high on the hindquarters, and carried in an arch over the dog's back. The legs are straight and slender, and the dog may or may not have dew claws on the front legs. The Papillon's feet are thin, straight, and elongated like those of a hare.

Papillons come in a variety of colors, but are always parti-color, or white with patches of color. An entirely white dog, or one with no white, is not considered ideal and will be disqualified from the show ring. If one or both ears are mostly or entirely white, the dog will also be severely penalized. The patches of color can be black, red, lemon, sable, or tri-color and their arrangement on the dog's body are not important to the breed standard. Most Papillons have a white muzzle and a blaze, or patch of white, on the forehead. Symmetrical markings on the face are desirable. The breed standard demands that they have dark eyes with black rims, as well as a deeply pigmented black nose and lips.

A Papillon's coat must be long, fine, silky, and straight. The breed does not have a double coat. The hair on the chest and hindquarters is profuse and the ears are well-fringed. The hair on the back of the front legs is long and flowing. The hair is short on the head, face, front of the front legs, and from the hocks down on the rear legs. The feet and toes also have short hair, but some dogs may have tufts of hair growing on the toes that form a point, like the feet of a hare.

Breed Behavioral Characteristics

"Papillons are a top obedience and performance dog. They are super smart, lively, and great retrievers."

Sally Howard
Tiny T Papillons / K's Klassic Ponies

Papillons are outgoing, affectionate little dogs that thrive on attention. They have been bred for hundreds of years as companion dogs and would prefer to spend every moment possible with their humans. Papillon owners joke that owning a Papillon means that you'll never go

Photo Courtesy of Madison Hall

FUN FACT
Dog Royalty

Marie Antoinette's favorite dog, named Coco, was an early version of the Papillon breed. It's said that at the end of Antoinette's life, she carried Coco to the guillotine, though this is likely only a legend. Coco survived the French Revolution and his grave can now be found in the gardens of the Hôtel de Seignelay in Paris.

to the bathroom alone again! If possible, Papillons would gladly spend every moment of their day with their humans. They also enjoy the company of other dogs, of course, but most Papillons would prefer to spend their time with people rather than other animals. Papillons also tend to prefer their own family over strangers, so if you have visitors, your Papillon will probably prefer to sit with you rather than with your visitor. This is not to say that Papillons are unfriendly, as quite the opposite is true. Papillons are friendly little dogs that love meeting new friends, but at the end of the day they'd rather cuddle with their family than with their friends.

Papillons are considered the eighth most intelligent breed, according to a study done by Stanley Coren, a professor in dog psychology at the University of British Columbia in Vancouver. This study reflects both the Papillon's intellect as well as their willingness to please their handler. Coren's study found that Papillons are among a select number of breeds who learn to repeat a behavior on demand with less than five repetitions and who, 95 percent of the time or better, obey a command on the first request. Amanda Vidrine of Earth Angels Papillons says, "They are so intelligent that it is like they can read your mind. When I talk to mine, I would swear that they understand." Many Papillon owners find that this intelligence is both a pro and con to Papillon ownership. The dogs are generally eager to please and quick to learn, but they can also find their way into trouble if their minds and bodies are not properly exercised.

Many small breeds of dogs have a reputation of being nervous, yappy, and insecure. Papillons, however, are more like a big dog in a small body. Each dog is an individual, and the way a dog was raised does have an impact on its personality, but most Papillons are confident and nearly fearless. As for the barking, Papillons are a quiet breed and rarely bark for no reason. Your dog will gladly let you know when you have visitors but will be relatively quiet most of the time. Papillons learn quickly when it is acceptable and not acceptable to bark.

Papillons are extremely playful little dogs that continue to act like puppies well into adulthood. These mischievous little dogs are always ready for a game, regardless of whether you are or not. It's not uncommon for Papillons to play 'keep-away' with their favorite toys or their owners' socks. Their lively manner can sometimes get them into trouble though. Papillons will gladly play with anyone who is willing, including bigger dogs that tend to play rough, so managing this tiny dog's big attitude is a big part of Papillon ownership.

Is a Papillon the Right Fit for You?

If you're looking for a small dog that will lounge around the house all day, the Papillon is probably not the breed for you. These lively dogs may be small, but they need adequate exercise to thrive. Papillons are intelligent, athletic little dogs that thrive on mental and physical stimulation. They make excellent competition dogs and are reg-

Photo Courtesy of
Aisling Murtagh

15

ularly seen in agility and obedience competitions. They love pleasing their handler and will quickly learn any new command. If you're looking for an active companion to keep you company on long walks, or would like to get into dog sports, the Papillon may be just what you're looking for.

The butterfly ears and flowing coat make the Papillon one of the most beautiful breeds of dogs, but be sure that the breed's beauty isn't the only thing enticing you to adopt one. Reflect on your own lifestyle and activity level before considering a Papillon. If you're looking for an ornamental dog that you can leave at home all day, you may need to consider a different breed. They are not an independent dog and would rather spend every moment of their day with their people. They do not do well in homes where they're left alone for long periods of time.

Papillons are not low-shedding or hypoallergenic dogs. They are a single-coated breed and therefore do not experience the heavy seasonal shedding of other breeds. However, they will shed consistently year-round. Feeding a high-quality diet can help minimize shedding, but be prepared to clean up after your Papillon. Regular brushing can also help keep the shedding under control. Luckily, Papillons do not require much grooming beyond regular brushing and the occasional bath.

If you have children, you need to consider whether a Papillon is the right dog for your household. Very young children can seriously injure a small dog simply because they don't understand their actions. Likewise, small children can also get hurt if your Papillon decides to defend himself. Papillons are confident, self-assured dogs that can and will defend themselves if they feel threatened. Typically, Papillons do better in households with older, more responsible children. Even older children should be supervised in the first few weeks or months of owning a Papillon. If they're used to dogs that they can roughhouse with, you may find that they will play too rough with such a petite dog. Children and dogs can become best friends, but just be cautious when considering bringing a Papillon into your home.

As with children, if you have other pets in your home it's important to consider how they'll react to having a frisky little dog in the house. Older pets may find a Papillon's energy to be too much for them and could become aggressive. Larger dogs may not injure a tiny dog on purpose, but they can easily hurt or even kill a Papillon by playing too rough, running into them, or knocking them over. If you have cats, make sure they're dog-friendly before adopting a Papillon. Papillons are at just the right level to be scratched and a cat's claw can seriously damage a Papillon's eye. You may find that you need a slower introduction when bringing such a petite breed into your house, so make sure your other pets will accept a new member of the family and don't rush the socialization. Papillons can also find themselves in trouble with farm animals or livestock. Their bold and fearless attitude can easily put them under the feet of a horse or in range of a goat that doesn't care for dogs. Some Papillons also have high prey drives, so they may need training and supervision when it comes to smaller animals such as chickens or rabbits. Make sure you're willing to commit the time and energy to ensuring that all members of your family, both human and animal, get along with your new Papillon. If not, you may need to reconsider whether a Papillon is the right breed for you.

CHAPTER 2
Choosing a Papillon

"When choosing a puppy listen to what either the breeder or rescue is telling you. Move past the fantasy of what your perfect Papillon has to be, and care more about if their temperament is one that works for your home. Color, sex, and size should have little importance when compared with your lifestyle, what current animals are in home, and your timeline."

Cherish Dewitt
Playtyme Papillons

Buying vs. Adopting

After making the decision to bring a Papillon into your household it's time to decide whether to buy your puppy from a reputable breeder or adopt from a shelter or rescue. Picturing your ideal dog can help you decide whether to buy or adopt. Are you looking for a future show dog or simply a loving companion? Karen Lawrence of MCK Papillons says, "Know what you want first. Some are very active, and some are happy to just sit in your lap." Narrowing down your goals for your new dog will help you to determine where to find your perfect Papillon.

Before you begin your search, decide whether you want a puppy or an adult. Adopting a puppy involves a lot of training and supervision. Raising a puppy can be an exciting experience for the whole family, but it is a lot of work. Puppies are not house-trained and explore the world with their mouth, often chewing on your furniture and belongings. However, a puppy is also a clean slate. You won't be inheriting any bad behavior from previous homes and you can train the dog as you like. Adult dogs, on the other hand, are past their chewing stage, are often already house-trained, and often require less work to integrate them into your household. Shelters or rescues are likely to have more adults to choose from, but breeders occasionally have retired show or breeding dogs available as well. If you decide on a puppy instead of an adult, be sure to check out your local Papillon rescue, as they may have puppies available for adoption.

After you've decided on the ideal age for your new dog, you need to consider what gender you'd prefer. If you have other dogs, they may have a preference for their new companion. It's not uncommon for two female dogs to have a difficult time getting along, so if you already have a female dog with a strong personality, you might consider getting a male Papillon. Likewise, if you have a male dog with a dominant personality, he may get along better with a female than a male. However, many dogs are happy to play with dogs of either gender, so it may be up to you to decide. Male and female dogs can differ in personality, so knowing what gender you prefer will help narrow down your search.

If you have a clear idea of what your new dog will look like, you may already know what color and coat pattern you're looking for. Unless you are dead set on having a dog of a certain color, keeping an open mind will allow you to find the perfect dog based on more important qualities such as age, gender, or temperament. Phalènes and Papillons are both great dogs, but now is the time to decide whether you prefer the drop ears of the Phalène or the erect ears of the Papillon.

Once you decide on your ideal dog, you'll have a better idea of where to find it. If you're looking for a competition dog with the perfect conformation or incredible athletic ability, a breeder will probably be your best choice. If you want a loving companion and you don't need a pedigree of champions, consider adopting from a shelter or breed rescue. You may want to look into both rescues and breeders to ensure that you have considered all options in your search for the perfect Papillon.

How to Find a Reputable Breeder

If you choose to buy your puppy from a breeder, it's important to carefully consider the breeder and not impulsively buy the first puppy you see for sale. Buying a puppy from a breeder who is passionate about improving the breed will give you a better chance of raising a healthy dog with no genetic diseases. Breeders will also have a thorough understanding of the parents' temperaments, personalities, and physical abilities.

A great way to find a reputable breeder is to attend a local dog show, especially if you intend to compete with your new Papillon. At the show, you'll be able to meet competitors and find out where they got their dogs. Most dog show contestants will be more than happy to talk about their dogs, and they may have breeders that they recommend, both locally and nationwide. Seeing the types of dogs that these breeders produce will also give you an idea of whether their dogs will suit your lifestyle.

If you're unable to attend a dog show, a simple internet search is a great way to find a reputable Papillon breeder. Many breeders keep their websites updated with their dogs' performance records, photographs, and health tests. They may also have available puppies listed or the dates of litters planned for the future. You'll be able to find their email address or phone number, so you can contact them to ask questions or set up a time to meet in person.

A reputable Papillon breeder should be happy to discuss their dogs and answer any questions you may have. They should have proof of all health tests and certifications as well as any show or performance records for their dogs. If a breeder seems hesitant to show you any documentation, it might suggest that they have something to hide. Breeders who are passionate about their breed will always be open and willing to talk in order to find the perfect home for their dogs. Be wary of any breeders who discourage you from visiting their home or kennel, or those who don't want you to meet the puppies' parents. Some breeders are cautious about bringing strangers into their homes with unvaccinated young puppies around, but they're likely more concerned about the health of their puppies rather than keeping secrets. Use your best judgment to determine whether you should trust this person. If you find the breeder to be open and trustworthy, make an appointment to meet them and their dogs to discuss what you're looking for.

If you're looking to raise a contender in conformation, agility, obedience, or any other sport, a breeder can help you choose the right puppy to meet your goals. You'll be able to see the parents themselves and examine both their health and competition records, as well as those of your future puppy's siblings. Cherish Dewitt of Playtyme Papillons says, "Breeders should be showing dogs in conformation and performance

Photo Courtesy of
Terryl Johnson

events and have titles on dogs in both areas. What this tells a buyer is that trainability, as well as structure, is important to a breeder. Even if they don't show their own dogs, someone should be."

Health Tests and Certifications

Photo Courtesy of Lacy Gillen

Reputable breeders regularly test their dogs for common genetic disorders to improve the health of the breed and reduce the frequency of genetic diseases and disorders known to affect their breed. If a dog does not pass health testing with a satisfactory rating, the breeder should have the dog spayed or neutered to prevent the disorder from being passed on to future generations. This also applies to dogs who are carriers of any disease, regardless of whether they show symptoms. A good breeder works hard to improve the breed with every generation, and health testing and certifications are an excellent way to keep track of these improvements.

The Orthopedic Foundation for Animals (OFA) is one of the leaders in canine genetic research. Their database contains the results of thousands of individual dogs of nearly every breed. Breeders and owners can have their dogs tested by their local veterinarian and submit the results to the OFA for examination for a nominal fee. For most tests, the OFA recommends the dog be fully grown, usually over the age of 12 months, though some tests are required to be done after the age of two years. Each breed has a list of recommended tests and the ages at which they should be performed.

The OFA Canine Health Information Center requires Papillons over the age of 12 months to receive a patellar luxation test and an eye examination, with a retest every two years by a board-certified ophthalmologist. Papillons must also undergo a third test of the owner or breeder's choosing. Options for the third test include congenital or advanced cardiac screening, a PRA1 DNA test, or an NAD DNA test. The DNA tests are for progressive retinal atrophy and neuroaxonal dystrophy, respectively. Once the dog has the required data on file, they are issued a Canine Health Information (CHIC) number and the results of those tests are made publicly available on the OFA website.

Breeder Contracts and Guarantees

According to Nicholas Forbes of DreamPaps Papillons, "Papillons are a healthy breed with very few health concerns when purchased from a reputable breeder that does health testing, provides a health guarantee, as well as offers a happiness warranty time period." Breeder contracts and guarantees are an essential part of purchasing a purebred puppy. These contracts will protect you and the breeder financially while keeping the puppy's well-being a priority. The contract will state the specific puppy you're adopting and the price you've agreed to pay, as well as any conditions of the adoption.

Typically, by signing a breeder's contract you're agreeing to take on the responsibility of the puppy's health and well-being. Many contracts include statements about required regular immunizations and health checks, as well as spaying or neutering at an appropriate age. Most breeders will require dogs adopted into pet homes to be spayed or neutered, typically at around six months of age. If you're planning to show or compete with your new Papillon, you may have a different agreement with your breeder as show dogs must remain intact. Sometimes, breeders will return a portion of the purchase price upon proof of spaying or neutering.

Certain breeders will also include clauses requiring you to feed a certain type of food. Breeders who are avid fans of raw diets will often only allow their dogs to go to families who intend to continue feeding raw food. Most breeders have been working with their breed for a long time and have found, through trial and error, what food works best for their dogs, and they frequently encourage their adopters to continue this diet to ensure the success and well-being of dogs no longer in their care.

Contracts should also contain a clause guaranteeing that the puppy is free from any significant genetic diseases or disorders. If a breeder has properly health tested their dogs, this risk is low, but it's still important to include this in the adoption agreement. Should a puppy test positive or show signs of a genetic abnormality, the contract should state what actions are to be taken by the breeder and adopter. Some adopters choose to keep their puppy regardless of any special needs, but others may choose to return the dog to the breeder. In the case of a puppy's death due to a disease originating from the breeder's care, the contract should guarantee either a refund or a replacement puppy from a future litter.

Photo Courtesy of
Judith Sattler

Most reputable breeders will also state that they are willing to take the dog back at any time and for any reason should you no longer be able to care for it. This is to prevent the dog from ending up in a shelter or an inappropriate home where it may face less than ideal conditions or even euthanasia. This portion of the contract may also include a 'happiness clause.' If you are not happy with your new Papillon for any reason, you may return it to breeder. Breeders who are passionate about their dogs would rather take the puppy back with no questions asked than risk the dog ending up in a shelter or an abusive or neglectful home.

Be sure to read the contract thoroughly and discuss any questions you may have with the breeder. Both parties need to agree before any legally binding paperwork is signed. Remember, these contracts protect both you and the breeder, as well as the puppy.

Choosing the Perfect Puppy

"Dogs have personalities just like people do. Find the right dog that appeals to your personality."

Amanda Vidrine
Earth Angels' – Chihuahuas and Papillons

Choosing the perfect puppy can be a daunting task, but a knowledgeable breeder can help you make the right decision. If you've already discussed your goals for your new puppy, you and your breeder can work together to find the right fit.

Cynthia Springer of Rocyn Papillons believes that a puppy's appearance should be the least of a potential adopter's concerns. She advises, "Do not get wrapped up with color or markings but look at temperament, especially of the parents if possible." While you may have a vision of the perfect puppy, your ideal match may not be exactly what you envisioned. Being open-minded about a dog's appearance will allow you to choose a puppy based on more important qualities, such as temperament and performance abilities.

If you're torn between two or more puppies in a litter, carefully examine each puppy. Even young puppies will display personality traits that will continue into adulthood. If you want a dog with a gregarious, sociable personality, pay attention to which puppy approaches you first. If you'd prefer a more laidback dog, look for one that would rather sit quietly on your lap than wrestle with her siblings but which does not show signs of fearfulness. Confidence and activity level are evident from just a few weeks of age, so knowing what you want from your ideal dog will help you to determine which puppy to take home. Again, seeking the breeder's opinion can help with your decision. The breeder has spent a lot of time with the puppies since they were born and has seen their personalities grow and develop, so he or she will know which puppy will best match your lifestyle.

FUN FACT
Lap of Luxury

Perhaps the richest Papillon (or dog for that matter!) is the late Lauren Bacall's dog, Sophie, who received an inheritance of $10,000 when the actress passed away in 2014.

Photo Courtesy of
Tara Donel

Tips for Adopting a Papillon

If you've chosen to adopt a Papillon from a shelter or rescue organization rather than from a breeder, you should still have an idea of what you're looking for in a companion. Most shelters and rescues put their dogs through a variety of tests to determine their personalities, ideal lifestyles, and any challenges potential adopters may face. However, some shelter environments can be stressful, and dogs may act differently than they would in a home. Many organizations place their dogs in foster homes, so their foster family will have a better idea of how the dog behaves in a home setting. Discuss your lifestyle and personality with the volunteers or foster families to determine which dog will suit you best.

Before adopting, you need to decide if you're willing to take on challenging behaviors. Many shelter dogs have developed bad habits or have simply never been taught manners, so they may need significant training. Make a list of which behaviors you're willing to work with and which behaviors are deal-breakers. Some habits, such as shyness and marking in the house, are relatively easy to correct, while more aggressive behaviors will require more serious training and dedication.

If you have children in your home, you'll need to discuss this with the rescue staff. Some Papillons are fearful or aggressive with children and it's important to make sure your new dog is comfortable around kids to prevent injuries or a return to the shelter.

If you have other pets, many organizations will require you to introduce your current pets to your potential new family member. Introducing pets on neutral territory, in a supervised environment, is an excellent way to make sure everyone gets along before you bring your new Papillon home. This can make the introduction at home less stressful and lessen the likelihood of any serious fights and subsequent injuries.

Some rescues will also require a home check by one of their volunteers. This is not something to worry about; they are simply making sure your home is a safe environment for a Papillon. If you've done your homework and properly puppy-proofed your home, you should have no problems. If the rescue volunteer does find something unacceptable about your home, they will likely give you a chance to fix the problem before you're approved for adoption.

CHAPTER 3:
Preparing Your Home for Your New Papillon

Adjusting Your Current Pets and Children

Introducing your new Papillon to your existing household may sound daunting, but with a little preparation, it can be done safely and relatively easily. Just remember, your current family members may need time to adjust to their new addition, and vice versa, so don't rush the introduction.

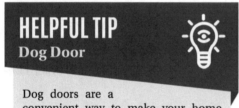

HELPFUL TIP
Dog Door

Dog doors are a convenient way to make your home more accessible for your dog, allowing him to go outside at will to play or relieve himself. But be cautious about leaving these doors unsecured at night. Nocturnal creatures, such as racoons, often make use of dog doors to enter homes. Unfortunately, they often have difficulty in finding the door when they want to leave. The Humane Society recommends locking dog doors at night or purchasing a door which only opens upon receiving a signal from a pet collar worn by your dog.

If you have a small area with minimal traffic such as a laundry or mudroom, you can set up a special area for your new dog to adjust to your household without stressing anyone out. To create a barrier that keeps everyone safe without isolating your new Papillon, you can install a removable gate. There are many safe options available on the market intended for both pets and babies. These gates are usually pressure-mounted, so they don't damage your walls or door frames. A small playpen or exercise pen works well, too. The idea is to create a barrier that will prevent any accidental injuries from aggression or rambunctious playing while still allowing the family and the new dog to see, hear, and smell each other. This way, current pets and children can familiarize themselves with the new Papillon for as long as he is comfortable. If your new family member feels overwhelmed, he can retreat to his bed or an area further away from the gate or playpen walls.

After your new Papillon has settled into his special area, you can begin introducing your existing family members. Introductions should hap-

Photo Courtesy of Tara Donel

pen one person or pet at a time, so no one feels too overwhelmed. Introductions should take place in a quiet, neutral area of your home. If your current dog spends a lot of time in the living room but hardly ever goes into the dining room, you may find that he'll be less territorial with the new addition in the dining room. If your pets are not allowed outside, indoor-only cats for instance, you'll find that a quiet area of the house will work best. If the weather permits, introducing the dogs outside, on neutral territory, is the best way to allow your family members to familiarize themselves. Introductions often go well and the new addition fits right into your family, but if there is tension between current pets and the new Papillon, don't rush it. They may need more time familiarizing themselves with the safety of the gate or playpen to protect them. Some pets prefer a slower introduction, especially when the new addition is an overly enthusiastic Papillon puppy.

After you've successfully introduced all members of your family, you can begin allowing your new dog more access to your home. At first, allow your Papillon access to one room at a time, and only under supervision. Your current pets may be territorial about certain areas of the house, so by observing all of their interactions during the first few weeks you can prevent any future problems they may have with sharing. If your new Papillon is not yet house-trained, you'll also be able to prevent any accidents that can interfere with his training.

Dangerous Things That Dogs May Eat

"You must keep a watchful eye on everything they can get into. Make sure all small items are picked up off the floor. They may chew electrical cords. Make sure plants in the house cannot be reached and are not poisonous to dogs."

Nana Ridgeway
Nanken Papillons

The average household can be full of poisonous or dangerous objects, so it's important to thoroughly puppy-proof your house before bringing your new addition home. Go through each room of your house and determine how easy it might be for your puppy to access any potential dangers.

Poisons intended for insects or rodents can be especially dangerous to curious new puppies. Dogs explore the world with their mouths, so they are likely to ingest anything they find interesting. If you have a pest problem, ask a professional for help dealing with the problem without the use of poison. There are many methods to control mice or insects that are much safer for dogs.

Another potentially deadly concern, especially if you're bringing home your new dog in the winter, is antifreeze. Antifreeze has a sweet taste, so pets readily lap up the toxic liquid when they find it. Be sure to clean up any spills and repair any leaks before allowing your dog in these areas. Leaks can also be deadly for other pets in the neighborhood so it's best to fix the problem before anyone gets hurt. If your dog does accidentally ingest something toxic, call your local veterinarian or poison control hotline immediately.

If you have children, be sure that no small toys or game pieces are left where your new dog could find them. These items can become a choking hazard or cause an intestinal blockage if ingested. In addition to being hazardous, your children can become upset with the dog if he chews up their favorite toy. So, to prevent any feuds or choking fatalities, it's best if your children tidy up once they're done playing. This also applies to your puppy's own toys. If any of his toys have been broken, torn, or chewed into smaller pieces, it's time to take them away before they can accidentally be swallowed. If your new dog is particularly destructive with toys, it may be best to only offer them when you can supervise playtime.

Photo Courtesy of Melanie Lawler

Outdoor gardens can become a dangerous area for dogs depending on the types of plants you grow. If your dog has access to the area, make sure there are no toxic plants that could be eaten. If you aren't willing to give up your beautiful but deadly plants, it would be wise to fence them off to prevent any tragedies. If you enjoy keeping houseplants, do your research to be sure that they aren't toxic to pets. Regardless of their toxicity, it's best to keep them out of reach to prevent potential tummy trouble or messes.

Many Papillons develop a bad habit of raiding the trash can, which can be a source of delicious and dangerous delights. If you've noticed your new dog paying extra attention to the trash can, you may need to find a new place to store your garbage. If you can't store your trash can in a dog-proof cabinet or closet, there are a variety of trash cans on the market that have locking lids and which are heavy enough to prevent small dogs from tipping them over.

Other Household Dangers

Photo Courtesy of Dawn Hammerle

If your home has a pool with a fence around it, make sure that the gate is closed at all times and that your Papillon cannot squeeze between the rails. It can take only a moment for a curious Papillon to find himself in a pool with no way out. If your pool doesn't have a fence, consider having one installed or only allow your dog to access the area with supervision. Even a dog who can swim well can panic and be unable to find the way out.

Another common household danger, especially for small dogs, is any long flight of stairs. Papillon puppies, and even some adults, are simply too small to safely manage more than a couple stairs at a time. Pressure-mounted baby gates are a great way of preventing accidents while still allowing human access to the stairs.

Power cords can also pose a danger to curious puppies exploring their new home. An electrical cord can easily be mistaken for an interesting chew toy to a young Papillon, so make sure all cords within your puppy's designated area are stowed above his reach.

Make sure all pesticides, cleaning products, and other household chemicals are kept out of reach. Papillons are curious dogs and can easily get into trouble if these types of products are left out. Beauty and hygiene products can also be harmful to dogs if ingested, so make sure your dog doesn't have access to your medications, deodorants, or hair products.

Preparing a Space for Your Dog Inside

The first step of preparing a space for your new Papillon is to choose a room in your home that will be dedicated to your dog for the few weeks or months. Many new dog owners opt for a laundry room, guest bathroom, or even the kitchen. Smaller spaces generally work better for puppies or adults that are not yet house-trained. Dogs don't like to relieve themselves too close to their eating or sleeping areas, so confined spaces tend to discourage them from making a mess. Regardless of the size of the room, your puppy is likely to make a few messes, so rooms with easy-to-clean floors, such as tile or linoleum, often work best. If possible, choose a room near the area where your family spends the most time. Your new dog will be able to watch the activities of your family without feeling so isolated.

Next, you'll need to thoroughly puppy-proof the area. Karen Lawrence of MCK Papillons suggests, "Get on the floor at the puppy's level and see what they can get into." Remove any dangers such as power cords, children's toys, or anything harmful your Papillon could eat or chew on. You'll need to make sure that the dog can't escape the area, so make sure any pressure-mounted gates or temporary barriers are installed correctly and a tiny Papillon can't squeeze through any gaps.

Once the area is safe, you can start setting up your supplies. First, lay out a few disposable puppy pads. These absorbent pads make cleanup a breeze. If you're bringing home a puppy or a rescue with an uncertain past, you'll have quite a few messes to clean up before he or she is fully house-trained, and it's much easier to pick up and dispose of a soiled puppy pad than it is to scrub a dirty floor. A puppy pad under food and water dishes can also help with cleanup if your Papillon is a messy eater. If you notice your new dog chewing up or destroying the puppy pads, you may have to take them away. If ingested, puppy pads can easily cause an intestinal blockage, which can be fatal without emergency surgery. So, if your new Papillon is a chewer, you may end up scrubbing the floor a few times, but it's better than a potential tragedy.

Many owners choose to set up their dog's bedding near the entrance to their dog's space. This is likely where your dog will be waiting for you or watching your activities, so it's a logical place to put a comfortable bed. Many Papillons enjoy burrowing under blankets, so providing a small blanket in addition to the bed will give your dog the option if this is something he enjoys. Keep an eye on your new pet, especially if you're bringing home a puppy. Many dogs enjoy chewing on bedding and will enthusiastically rip all the stuffing out of their cushy new bed. This can become a choking hazard or put the dog at risk for an intestinal blockage, so if your dog destroys bedding, you may have to find another bedding choice. There are many beds on the market made of tougher material to discourage chewing, so find what works for you and your dog.

Be sure to set up the food and water dishes some distance away from the bedding to prevent a wet or soiled sleeping area. You may also want to set them away from the entrance to your dog's area. If your new dog is enthusiastic about greeting the family, he may accidentally knock over the dishes in his excitement. Remember, your dog should have access to clean water at all times, so keep an eye on the bowl and refill it if it gets knocked over.

Preparing Outside Spaces

If your home has an outside space, such as a yard or garden, you need to make sure it's safe for your new family member before you bring the puppy home. Just as you did indoors, look at the yard from your dog's perspective.

Walk the perimeter of your property, making sure there are no holes or gaps in your fence where a Papillon could squeeze through. The outside world is a dangerous place for an unaccompanied Papillon puppy. Papillons are small enough to be at risk of being taken by wild animals or stray dogs, and most drivers won't see such a small dog if it ends up in the street. Keeping your dog safely within the confines of your yard will keep him safe from such dangers.

If your property has a pool, you'll need to make sure it's fenced off and your dog can't squeeze through the gaps. Most pool fencing is made to prevent children from squeezing through, not small dogs. If you think your dog can fit between the bars, don't worry, you don't need to replace the entire fence. Many Papillon owners have found success in lining the lower half of their pool fence with chicken wire or garden fencing. The wire fencing also discourages chewing, so it's unlikely your Papillon will be able to get through.

If your yard is landscaped, or you have a vegetable or flower garden, make sure the plants are not toxic to dogs. If you find that your yard has toxic plants, promptly remove them or fence them off. Some dogs, especially puppies, will gobble up fallen leaves or even stems or berries if they find them. With a little work, your Papillon should be able to safely explore your yard full of non-toxic plants.

Photo Courtesy of
Silvia Gold

Supplies

Making a supply list and checking it twice will prevent any last-minute panic when you bring home your new Papillon and realize you forgot to buy food or puppy pads. If you have other dogs in your home, you likely won't need to buy everything, but it's a good idea to buy a few new items for your new dog in case your other dogs become territorial or have trouble sharing.

Ask the breeder or shelter what your Papillon is currently eating. If the food is not what you'd like to feed your new dog, ask if they can provide you with a few days' worth of meals. Switching foods quickly can cause digestive upset, so you'll need some of the old food to slowly mix with the new food to make a smooth transition. If the dog is a rescue, find out if he has any food sensitivities or allergies, so you'll be able to purchase the appropriate food. This information will also help you choose treats. Training should begin as soon as you bring your dog home, so be prepared. Most dogs are at least somewhat food motivated, so choose something small, easy to eat, and especially delicious.

Depending on the age and size of your dog, you'll need to buy an appropriately sized collar and leash. Most collars are adjustable, so you should be able to estimate the correct size. Whether you prefer glitz and glamour, or something subtler, your local pet store or favorite online retailer will have a nearly endless variety of choices. Whatever your choice, be sure you pick up an identification tag with your current phone number or address. These tags are usually available in a variety of sizes, so you should be able to find one appropriate for a Papillon.

A comfortable bed is one of the most important items in helping your dog settle into his new home. Choose a bed that's appropriate for the size of your Papillon. Small puppies may struggle with climbing into a lofty bed, while adult dogs will need enough room to sprawl out. Try to find a bed with a removable cover. There may be times that you'll need to wash the entire bed, but if it's only the surface that's soiled, it's much easier to unzip the cover and toss it in the wash. Many Papillons also enjoy burrowing into blankets, so consider purchasing a small blanket to place on top of their bed. Fleece blankets are an inexpensive, easy-to-wash option.

If you plan on purchasing toys for your new dog, decide on toys that are safe and appropriate for small dogs. Many puppies will choose to chew on inappropriate items while teething, so giving them another option can spare your shoes and furniture. Toys should be big enough that your dog is not likely to swallow them, but not so big that your puppy can't carry them around. Keep an eye on the toys and discard anything that has been torn or chewed, especially any small pieces that could become a hazard. Whether your dog prefers fetch over quiet chew time, or a good game of tug of war, you'll be able to find the perfect toy at your local pet store or favorite online retailer.

Even if you plan on taking your new Papillon to a professional groomer on a regular basis, you'll need a few grooming supplies for at-home maintenance. The most important item is a comb or brush. Papillons are known for their beautiful coats, but those gorgeous locks can tangle, so regular brushing is important. You may also want a shampoo and conditioner in case your puppy gets dirty or starts to smell. If you plan on trimming your dog's nails yourself, invest in a quality nail trimmer or grinder. If you have any doubts about what to buy, ask your local groomer for recommendations. Most groomers would be happy to suggest which tools are best for at-home coat care.

If you're bringing home a puppy, or an adult who is not yet house-trained, you'll need a few items to help with house-training. Absorbent, disposable puppy pads are great for keeping messes at a minimum, as well as to allow your dog to have an appropriate place to relieve himself while you're away. Many Papillon owners choose to train their dogs to use these pads while they're at work, or during bad weather, when outdoor walks are not possible. Some Papillon owners even train their dogs to use litter boxes. Cleaning supplies are also an important part of your house-training tool kit. There are many cleaners available on the market that are made specifically for pet messes and include certain enzymes to help eliminate odor and discourage any future marking in that same spot. If you're worried about whether your new Papillon will tell you when he or she needs to go out, you can purchase bells to hang on or near your doors. Most dogs learn very quickly that nudging or pawing at the bells will get your attention to let them outside.

CHAPTER 4
Bringing Home Your New Papillon

The Importance of Having a Plan

Photo Courtesy of
Terryl Johnson

Having a thorough plan for bringing home your new Papillon will make the transition smoother and less stressful for both your family and your new dog. If you bring your new companion home and realize you don't have the proper supplies and don't know where your Papillon will spend the first night, it can create a chaotic and stressful environment. Thoroughly planning the arrival of your new dog will minimize the stress for both of you and hopefully make the introduction a positive experience.

If you have other dogs, or have previously had dogs, you may already have the experience to cope with any problems that arise. However, if you are a new dog owner, experiencing problems with your new dog within the first few days and weeks can lead to panic. Having a plan and being able to refer to it when necessary will give you a resource to go to when things aren't going as planned. For instance, if you plan your car ride home, you won't be upset or unprepared when your dog becomes car sick. If you've already purchased the necessary supplies, you'll be ready for cleanup when your puppy has its first accident in the house. Bringing a new family member home can be a stressful event, but being prepared and having a plan can make this exciting time more pleasant for the whole family.

The Ride Home

This may be your Papillon's first time in a car, so ensuring that it's a good experience for everyone will set the tone for future trips in the car. You may be excited about finally bringing your new family member home, but it's important to stay calm throughout the drive. Your dog won't understand that your elevated emotions are due to him, not due to the car, and he may show signs of anxiety or panic.

Photo Courtesy of Liz Krueger

An unrestrained dog in the car can be an accident waiting to happen. Depending on the age and size of your new Papillon and previous experiences with cars, there are several options for safe restraint. Older, more experienced dogs can be fitted with a harness and seat belt to keep them in place until you've arrived home safely. If your Papillon is young, or you're not sure about its previous experiences, a kennel may be your best option. Papillons are small dogs and appropriately sized kennels fit easily into most vehicles. If you'd prefer, there are many mesh or metal barriers on the market that will prevent your dog from jumping into the front seat where it can become a hazard to the driver.

Be prepared for any possible car sickness with your new dog. Even experienced travelers can become sick on occasion, so invest in seat covers, or bring along a few towels in case your Papillon becomes ill during the drive. If you've set up a crate in the car, lining it with a few washable towels or blankets will allow for easy cleanup when you get home.

Some dogs react badly when riding in the car for the first time. They may bark, cry, or even try to escape. Placing the dog in a kennel for the duration of the trip can help calm him while also keeping him safely restrained. Some dogs do well with a blanket or towel draped over their kennel to give them a sense of security. Again, remaining calm is essential to this important training opportunity. If you become anxious, your dog may become even more upset. If your breeder or foster family allows it, try bringing along your dog's favorite toy or blanket. The familiar smell can be soothing and may give the dog a sense of comfort in an otherwise stressful event.

The First Night Home

"Expect the pup will howl when he is left alone. They are so people oriented that they do not do well without their human companion. They will let you know."

Amanda Vidrine
Earth Angels' – Chihuahuas and Papillons

For your Papillon's first night home, it's best if you don't have any early appointments the next morning since it may not be a particularly restful night, especially if you're bringing home a puppy. This will be your puppy's first night away from his mother and littermates, so he may be somewhat distressed. If you're bringing home an adult dog, it can still be an upsetting change for him, especially if he's gotten used to a foster home or has come from a breeder's home.

Photo Courtesy of
Alexandra Perry

Where you have your Papillon spend his first night can have a big impact on how upset he gets. It may be tempting to put him somewhere out of earshot, so you can rest peacefully, but the isolation will probably cause him to howl and squeal throughout the entire night. Even if your long-term plan is for your dog to sleep in bed with you or on his own bed on the floor, it may be wise to have your dog sleep in a crate until you can fully trust him in the house. This way, you can put the crate somewhere near your own bed, so he knows he's not alone.

Be sure to take your dog outside to go to the bathroom as late as possible before you go to bed. You will also need to take him out first thing in the morning, so plan on taking him outside immediately after waking up. Depending on the age of your dog, you may also need to take him out at some point during the night. It may take some time for you to determine the difference between cries for attention and cries to go outside, but most young puppies will have to relieve themselves every few hours, even at night.

It may be difficult, but it's important to ignore your Papillon's initial cries once you put him in the crate to sleep. You can be assured that he doesn't have to go to the bathroom if you've just taken him out, so it is probably just upset about the situation. It may be hard to ignore a crying puppy, but the more you react to his cries, the more he'll howl to get your attention. Eventually, he'll settle down and realize it's time for sleep. If the puppy begins crying again in the middle of the night, it's safe to assume he has to relieve himself so it's best to take him outside as soon as possible.

The First Vet Visit

Since your dog will be visiting the vet on a regular basis for its entire life, it's important that the first visit is a good experience for everyone. Regardless of whether your dog is ready for his next round of vaccines, you should take him to visit your local veterinarian within a few days of bringing him home. Many breeders require this in their contracts, but it's generally considered a good idea to make sure your new Papillon is happy and healthy.

During your dog's first visit, your veterinarian will weigh your dog to determine if he is an appropriate weight for his age and size. He will then listen to your Papillon's heart and lungs, followed by checking his temperature. Next, a physical examination will determine if your dog's eyes, ears, teeth, skin, and abdomen are all in good health. The vet may ask if your dog is eating, drinking, and eliminating normally. If you have any concerns about your puppy's health, now is the time to mention them.

If your dog is due for vaccines, your veterinarian will discuss which vaccines are needed at this time and when you should bring your dog back for the next round. Your veterinarian should also explain any potential reactions your dog may have to the vaccines. Although most dogs receive their regular shots without problems, if your dog shows any reaction such as hives, swelling, or difficulty breathing, bring your dog back to the veterinary clinic immediately for treatment.

As part of his first physical, your Papillon may undergo a fecal test to determine if he has any intestinal parasites. Even if your dog isn't showing symptoms, it's generally standard procedure to test new patients, especially puppies, for parasites. Roundworms are especially common in

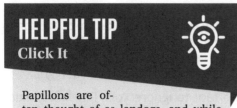

HELPFUL TIP
Click It

Papillons are often thought of as lapdogs, and while their small size may make it tempting to allow them to roam about the car while you're driving, this is an unsafe practice, not only for the driver but for the dog as well. One option to keep your dog safe while riding in the car is a dog seatbelt. Look for a seatbelt that has been crash test certified by an organization such as the Center for Pet Safety.

puppies but are easy to treat. If your puppy tests positive for parasites, you may have to give him several doses of deworming paste or tablets, but most puppies handle this treatment with little concern.

Your veterinarian may talk to you about microchipping your puppy. This procedure involves inserting a microchip, about the size of a grain of rice, beneath the dog's skin above the withers. This microchip can be scanned by any approved scanner which will then display a unique number that will allow the person scanning your dog to look up your contact information. Although this procedure is not required in most places, it's a convenient way to make sure your dog can find his way back to you if he disappears without his collar and identification tags and gets lost.

The first visit is a great time to discuss spaying and neutering with your veterinarian. They'll be able to recommend what age and weight your puppy should be before undergoing any procedure. They'll also be able to give you an idea of the cost of the surgery, so you can be prepared when the time comes. Many pet owners can be nervous about the idea of their beloved pet being anesthetized, so if you have any concerns, mention them to your veterinarian and he or she will be able to explain the procedure in detail and answer any questions you may have.

Puppy Classes

Puppy classes are basic obedience classes intended to teach young dogs basic manners, such as walking on a leash without pulling and coming when called. Many new owners struggle with getting their excited young Papillon to focus, so working with a professional trainer is a great way to begin your relationship with your new dog. In addition to learning the basic commands of sit, down, and stay, puppy classes are a great place to get advice on house-training and good manners.

Most puppy classes will require your Papillon to be a certain age before beginning training. This is for the health and safety of your dog as well as the others in the class. The age requirements are meant to ensure that puppies have had at least one round of vaccines and deworming before socializing with other dogs. Parasites and disease can spread quickly among puppies who haven't yet built up a strong immunity, so most trainers will ask for proof of vaccinations before allowing you and your puppy to come to class.

Depending on the area in which you live, you'll likely have plenty of choices for puppy classes. From formal obedience schools to individual trainers, do your research and talk to a few trainers before signing up. If you've purchased your Papillon from a breeder, he or she may have recommendations as well. Many shelters or rescues organize relatively low-cost puppy classes as a way of helping the community care for their dogs. If you aren't quite sure you're ready for puppy classes, you can also have a trainer visit your home to help you with basic commands until you're ready for obedience classes.

If you've brought home an adult Papillon, the same businesses and trainers that offer puppy classes should also offer basic obedience classes for adult dogs. Even adult dogs should be up-to-date on vaccines before arriving at their first class. If your Papillon has any serious behavioral problems, you may need to discuss them with your trainer. Group classes can be overwhelming to under-socialized dogs or those with aggression issues, so your trainer may recommend private lessons to begin with.

Obedience classes are also a great place to socialize your new Papillon in a safe, controlled environment. Proper socialization can prevent your dog from becoming fearful or aggressive with new people or dogs in the future. It also teaches your dog to focus on you and listen to your commands in any environment, not just at home. Socializing your dog will also help his confidence when introduced to new places and situations. Your Papillon will want to accompany you everywhere you go, so it's important to ensure that he'll approach new experiences with confidence and good manners.

Cost Breakdown for the First Year

The first year of dog ownership can be costly, so if you're living paycheck to paycheck, you may need to reconsider bringing a dog into your household. However, even on a tight budget, with proper planning and preparation, the cost of dog ownership can be managed.

If you choose to adopt your Papillon from a rescue organization or shelter, you'll likely pay an adoption fee, which helps cover the costs of care provided before the adoption. This fee can range anywhere from $50 to $350 or more, depending on the area, organization, and care given to the dog. Many rescues require their dogs to be spayed or neu-

Photo Courtesy of Casey Williams

tered prior to adoption and they are generally updated on any necessary vaccines.

If you choose to purchase your Papillon from a breeder, you may pay anywhere from $800 to several thousand dollars. This price can vary based on the breeder's health testing and guarantees, the parents' performance records, and the show or performance potential of the individual puppy. Breeders will also have given the puppies at least one round of vaccines.

The initial cost of the dog will be the least of your financial concerns. Supplies and routine veterinary care are mandatory expenses for all dog owners and can add up quickly. Depending on the average costs in your area and your choices in food and supplies, these costs can range from $815 to $2730, not including the initial adoption fee or purchase price. Here's a breakdown of the potential cost of dog ownership in the first year:

Mandatory Expenses	Cost Estimate
Food	$150 - $500
Food and Water Dishes	$10 - $50
Treats	$50 - $100
Toys	$20 - $200
Collars and Leashes	$10 - $100
Crate	$25 - $75
Dog Beds	$25 - $100
Vaccines and Routine Veterinary Care	$100 - $350
Heartworm Testing	$10 - $35
Heartworm Prevention	$25 - $125
Flea and Tick Prevention	$40 - $200
Spaying or Neutering	$150 - $400
Puppy Classes	$200 - $500
Total	**$815 - $2730**

Your potential costs within the first year are not just limited to basic supplies and care. If you choose to take your Papillon to a professional groomer, you must be prepared to spend approximately $25 to $65 every six to eight weeks. Many owners are more than happy to let a professional handle their dog's grooming needs, but just remember to factor this expense into your budget.

Photo Courtesy of
Leah Radley

If you plan on traveling without your Papillon, you must also consider the cost of hiring a pet sitter or boarding your dog at a kennel or boarding facility. Depending on your area and the level of care, this can be upwards of $50 per day. Of course, if you have friends or family who are dog lovers, you may be able to ask them to care for your Papillon in your absence.

The biggest potential expense to be prepared for is emergency veterinary care. As a pet parent, you will do your best to keep your Papillon safe and healthy, but accidents can and do happen. Emergency veterinary care can range from just a few hundred dollars to several thousand. Many dog owners choose to set aside money on a regular basis to help cover the cost of emergencies.

Possible Expenses	Cost Estimate
Professional Grooming	$150 - $600
Emergency Veterinary Services	$200 - $1000+
Pet Sitting or Boarding	$15 - $50+ per day

This section is not intended to scare you away from dog ownership; it's simply meant to prepare you for the financial burden of caring for an animal. Bringing a Papillon into your home is a big responsibility, so you need to carefully consider whether you're willing to spend the money necessary to proper care. Careful planning and budgeting can help you provide the best care possible without putting unnecessary strain on your finances.

CHAPTER 5
Being a Puppy Parent

"A Papillon is truly a big dog in a small package - so trainable and very much the companion with a 'willing to please' attitude."

Elyse Vandermolen
Clearlake Papillons

Standing by Your Expectations

Photo Courtesy of Elsa Rún Árnadóttir

When bringing a Papillon into your home it's important to be realistic about your expectations for yourself and your puppy. Cherish Dewitt of Playtyme Papillons says, "It's a lot more work than you realize. Puppies are a full-time commitment, so make sure you have enough time to devote to their development. The more time you have available, the faster you will house-train and teach other good behavior." You can't expect your Papillon to learn the rules of the house if you're not willing to take the time to teach them.

For the first few weeks, you shouldn't expect too much from your puppy. Remember, this is a new experience for both your puppy and your family, so while it's important to focus on training right away, you also need to be patient as everyone gets to know each other. If you set your expectations too high, you may be disappointed in your puppy's progress and behavior. Understand that you're essentially bringing home a tiny canine toddler and patience is key to his development and education.

How to Crate Train

Crate training is essential to any dog's life. Even if you don't plan on crating your Papillon as an adult, it's best to get him used to it anyway. He'll eventually experience being crated at the vet or groomer, and you don't want him panicking during an already worrisome situation. Dogs who haven't been properly crate trained often bark incessantly and relieve themselves out of stress. It's not uncommon for these dogs to dig or chew at the door, potentially causing injury to their teeth or paws. To prevent any unnecessary stress or injury to your dog in the future, it's important to teach him that the crate is a pleasant place to be.

HELPFUL TIP
Choosing a Crate

When choosing a crate for training your dog, it's important to choose a crate that is neither too big nor too small. The crate should be large enough for your dog to stand up fully and lie down comfortably. If the crate is too large, your dog may designate one side as his or her bathroom, leaving the rest of the crate as a clean sleeping area, thus defeating your house-training agenda.

Crate training will be easier if your dog learns to enjoy his time there, so make sure his crate is located somewhere quiet and out of the way. To ensure his crate is a place where he'll want to relax, make it as comfortable as possible. Place his favorite bed or blanket in there, and even his favorite toy, if you're sure won't destroy it in your absence. You can also leave the crate door open while you're home, to give him the option of lying in there whenever he wants.

To get your dog comfortable with being in the crate, encourage him to step inside on his own by tossing a few treats inside. Once he's comfortable going inside, you can start shutting the door behind him. Begin with just a few seconds at a time and then a few minutes. Eventually, you can start backing away from the crate for short periods of time while working up to stepping out of the room entirely. If your dog starts to bark or cry, do not let him out immediately. This will only reward his bad behavior. Instead, wait for him to quiet down before opening the door. With patience and encouragement, your dog will come enjoy the peace and quiet of his crate.

Chewing

Photo Courtesy of Danielle Grenier

Chewing is a dangerous habit for a Papillon to develop, but it's an unavoidable stage in a puppy's life. Remember, puppies explore the world around them by tasting and chewing everything. At around 16 weeks of age, your Papillon will also start to lose his puppy teeth as his adult teeth come in. This can cause discomfort which the puppy will try to relieve with chewing. Puppies will often chew inappropriate objects at this time, such as shoes, children's toys, and even furniture. If given the opportunity, they'll also chew dangerous items such as electrical cords or small items that they can choke on or swallow.

If your Papillon is chewing on an object you can't remove from the environment, such as the corners of walls or countertops, you may want to try using a chewing deterrent spray. There are many different types available on the market, but most are either spicy pepper or bitter apple flavored. Dogs are less likely to chew on an object that leaves an unpleasant taste in their mouth, so most owners find success relatively quickly. The spray will likely need to be reapplied fairly often until the puppy learns to leave the object alone.

To encourage your Papillon puppy to chew on more appropriate items around the house, be sure to provide him with a variety of safe chew toys. Your local pet store or favorite online retailer will have a vast assortment of toys that are perfect for a teething puppy. Some toys can even be frozen to provide cooling relief for your Papillon's sore gums. As always, monitor your puppy's chew toys to make sure no small pieces have been broken off or chewed down to a size that can be swallowed.

Growling and Barking

Papillons are confident little dogs who like to take charge, so it's not uncommon for a puppy to display aggressive behavior such as growling or barking. Puppies may also bark or growl in situations where they feel insecure or unsure. It may seem cute and harmless when your puppy is a tiny ball of fluff, but it can turn into a real problem if this behavior isn't corrected.

If your puppy growls or barks at people or other animals, clap your hands loudly to distract him. Do not try to comfort your Papillon in these situations as it can be interpreted as encouragement. Once the puppy stops growling and displays the correct behavior, you can reward with praise or treats. As your puppy grows and socializes more, you'll likely have to correct this behavior less often.

Digging

Digging is a bad habit that many puppies develop during their quest to explore their environment. Some breeds are more prone to digging than others, terriers for example, but any dog can develop this behavior. Dogs that dig sometimes ingest dirt, rocks, or sticks, and can break or rip their nails off. They may also be able to dig under your fence and escape your yard. However, most of the time it's just an eyesore on your landscaping.

The best way to discourage digging is to supervise your Papillon any time he goes outside. When you see him start to dig, clap your hands loudly to distract , just as you would if you caught him relieving himself in the house. After being corrected enough, your dog will lose interest in digging and go find something else to do. If you allow him to wander the yard unsupervised and only enforce the rules part of the time, you'll find it much more difficult to break the habit.

Separation Anxiety

Papillons would love to spend every minute of their day with their humans, so it's not uncommon for them to develop separation anxiety when left alone. Symptoms can include excessive barking, panting, pacing, and drooling. Some dogs also exhibit destructive behavior such as chewing up furniture and bedding or relieving themselves indoors. If confined to a certain area, they may also try to escape. This can easily become a dangerous situation, but it is easily

Photo Courtesy of Donna Murphy

Photo Courtesy of
Rebecca Johnson

solved. However, if you are struggling to find a solution to your Papillon's separation anxiety, consider discussing the matter with a professional dog trainer.

The most important step in preventing separation anxiety is not making a big deal about leaving or entering the house. Long goodbyes and enthusiastic hellos will only excite your dog and stress him out. It can be hard to leave the house without giving your adorable puppy a heartfelt goodbye, but in the end, he'll learn not to worry when you leave and will know that you'll be home soon. The same applies to greeting your dog when you come home. If you excitedly greet your dog and allow him to jump all over you, he's going to understand that your arrival or departure is an event he needs to be concerned about. Enter your house calmly, put your things away, and only greet your dog once he's calmed down.

Some Papillons may do better when they're left with animal companions. Knowing that they have another dog or cat at home with them will comfort them in your absence. Remember, dogs are pack animals and will almost always find comfort in their pack, even if it consists of animals other than dogs. If you work long hours and have no other animals, you may consider adopting another animal to keep your Papillon company in your absence.

If your Papillon has been crate trained, you may try crating him while you're gone. Some dogs find comfort in their own space and will behave more calmly when crated. However, if your dog has not been crate trained, crating can cause even more stress and he may even injure himself trying to escape the confines of the crate. You will know how your dog will react, so use your best judgement in this situation.

Running Away

Running away can be a dangerous habit for a Papillon to develop. Papillons are small and fast which means they can bolt out a door before you can do anything about it. Even if your dog only runs away from you in the house, it's still considered bad manners and should be dealt with immediately. Consult a professional trainer if you can't seem to break this potentially deadly habit.

If your dog has a habit of running away in the house or dashing out an open door, try leaving a leash on him while he follows you around the house. Dragging a leash around won't bother him as he runs around the house, but it will give you a chance to catch him before he escapes or runs from you.

The most important skill a Papillon can learn is a solid recall. Teaching your dog to come when you call, no matter what, could save his life someday. Begin training in the house with few distractions and work up to practicing in your yard, and eventually in public places. You may have a friend or family member help you with this. Investing in a long leash can help make practice easier and safer.

Bedtime

To encourage your dog to go to sleep at bedtime, try to keep him calm in the hours before you go to bed. Don't take him outside for a game of fetch or try to teach him new tricks. Try to accomplish those tasks earlier in the day to wear him out. The busier you keep your Papillon during the day and the more exercise he gets, the calmer he's going to be around bedtime.

Remember to take your Papillon outside for a potty break right before bed, especially if you're still working on house-training. The later you're able to take him out, the more likely it is that he'll be able to make it through the night without having to go outside. Many Papillons understand that it's bedtime after their last trip outside and will readily go to bed when brought back inside. Develop a routine and you'll find that getting ready for bed will become easier.

Photo Courtesy of
Leah Radley

Where your dog sleeps will depend on where he is with his house-training as well as on your personal preference. Whether your Papillon puppy sleeps in a crate, playpen, or a dog bed, he should be allowed to sleep near your own bed. Being in the presence of his family will help your puppy relax and sleep through the night.

Leaving Your Dog Home Alone

The first few times you leave your Papillon home alone can be stressful for both of you. Preparation is key to creating a good experience and discouraging bad habits. Make sure your puppy is secure in a safe area that she cannot escape from. Whether you choose a crate, playpen, or a specific room, thoroughly check the area for any potential dangers. Even if you've already puppy-proofed the area, take one more look to make sure everything is as it should be.

During the first few days and weeks with your puppy, try leaving him in his designated area for short periods of time while you're home. This will allow him to get used to the space without being left alone. With enough practice, he'll be comfortable in his space whether you're at home or away.

Remember, the key to preventing separation anxiety is to quietly leave the house and calmly enter. If you don't make a big deal out of leaving, your dog won't either. Your puppy will grow up to be a much more well-adjusted adult if he understands that when you walk out the door, it's not the end of the world. Upon returning to the house, only acknowledge your dog once he's calmed down. Eventually, you'll be able to go to work or to run errands without having to worry about your Papillon.

Photo Courtesy of Lynne Rotan

CHAPTER 6
House-Training

"Set up a small fenced in safe area to teach house training. Don't allow full access to house but keep them in same room with you so you are aware of what they are doing. If you don't have time to be training place the puppy in their safe area. Dogs are always learning, either good or bad behaviors. Your job as a new puppy owner is to work on positive learning."

Cherish Dewitt
Playtyme Papillons

Different Options for House-training

Before you bring your Papillon home and begin house-training, consider your options for house-training. Which methods will you use while your puppy is learning, and which will you use when your Papillon becomes an adult? Papillons are small, intelligent dogs and can easily be trained to use a litter box or indoor potty patch. They also quickly learn to use disposable puppy pads when needed. If you live in a particularly harsh climate, it may be difficult to take your Papillon for walks at certain times of the year, so litter-box training may be an option to consider using even after your puppy reaches adulthood. Use your best judgment and your own personal preferences and keep these goals in mind as you teach your Papillon the rules of the house.

Traditional house-training involves taking your puppy outside every few hours and teaching him that the only appropriate place to relieve himself is outside. If this is the method you'd prefer to use as an adult, you should focus on this while training your dog. If you're un-

HELPFUL TIP
Umbilical Training

Umbilical training is a constant supervision method of training which requires owner and dog to be attached to one another by a leash. This physical bond helps to avoid any accidents by allowing you to keep your attention constantly on your puppy.

sure, you can try using litter boxes or puppy pads while your Papillon is still young and unable to hold it for long periods of time. As he grows and can go longer between trips outside, you can phase out the indoor house-training accessories.

Litter boxes are a great indoor house-training option for toy dogs. Papillons learn quickly, and even young puppies understand how to use litter boxes after just a few tries. After years of litter-box training her puppies, Sally Howard of Tiny T Papillons says, "If the litter box is available while playing in the house, many times [the puppy] will run to the box to potty." Some owners use litter boxes intended for cats, while others use specially designed boxes for dogs or ferrets that have a higher back wall. As for the litter, there are specially designed litters for dogs available that are made from recycled paper or wood pulp. Some owners simply choose to use cat litter, so decide what works best for you and your Papillon.

Disposable puppy pads are another option to provide your dog with a place to go indoors. These absorbent pads can simply be picked up and thrown away when soiled. These are an especially convenient option to provide young puppies while they are still learning other methods of house-training. Older dogs can easily be trained to use them as well. Puppy pads are also a suitable long-term option if you intend to travel with your dog or would simply like to provide him with a place to go in case he can't wait until you return home.

The First Few Weeks

"Prevention of accidents is the key. Take them out, or to the potty pad, every couple of hours, especially after they eat and nap. In my experience a pup gets to about 5 months old and hits a growth stage where they might regress on their house training. Be ready to start over with the training. This stage only lasts about two weeks."

Cynthia Springer
Rocyn Papillons

Photo Courtesy of Terryl Johnson

The first few weeks are essential to any Papillon's house-training. Karen Lawrence of MCK Papillons advises, "Be consistent, and get them out often." The more consistent you are with training, the quicker your dog will learn. Initially, you will need to take your dog out every few hours. Papillons, like most toy breeds, are notoriously difficult to house-train. It takes patience and consistency, but it can be done.

The younger your dog, the more frequently he will need to go outside. The rule of thumb is that your puppy will be able to hold it for one hour for every month of his age. For instance, a three-month-old puppy should be able to go three hours before needing a break. Waiting much longer than this will guarantee an accident in the house. This rule even applies at night, so be prepared for some sleepless nights for the first few weeks. Once you develop a routine, you'll be able to better anticipate when your dog needs to go out, and accidents will become less frequent.

Positive Reinforcement

One of the quickest and most popular training methods for dogs is positive reinforcement. This method involves rewarding the dog when she performs a favorable behavior. Each time the dog repeats the behavior, it's reinforced with a positive stimulus, such as praise or food. The dog eventually learns that he can earn the reward by doing certain tasks. Papillons are particularly intelligent dogs, and with positive reinforcement, they can learn a new behavior with just a few repetitions.

Photo Courtesy of Kristina Klamborowski

Consistency is key with positive reinforcement. You want the dog to associate the treats and praise with going potty, not with going outside. Outside may be for playtime, too, but you want to set clear boundaries with house-training. When you first take your Papillon outside, try to stay calm and quiet while you command him to "go potty." He may want to play, but he needs to understand that he needs to go to the bathroom first, so ignore any attempts to engage in play. As you ask your dog to go potty, be prepared to reward him as soon as he relieves himself. It's best to stick with quiet verbal praise while he's going as you don't want to distract him. Once he's finished, you can lavish him with attention and tasty morsels and play until he's tired out.

Whether you choose to reward your dog will depend on his personality and food drive. Some dogs will do anything for a treat, while others would prefer to be the object of your affections. If you do choose to use food as a reward, make sure it's something that your dog absolutely loves. High-value treats will encourage your dog to repeat the desired behavior. Most treats intended for use during training are quite small, so that they can be fed to the dog without disrupting the training. The tiny treats let the dog know he's done a good job, but don't require him to take the time to chew the food or search for crumbs. However, it's okay to use bigger rewards for house-training. You want your dog to

Photo Courtesy of Archa Emerson

know he's done a good job, and this type of training allows for extra time during the reward. Don't give him too big of a snack though; it may satiate him and discourage him from repeating the behavior in a few hours.

If you choose to reward your dog with praise only, make a big deal out of it. When he relieves himself in the correct spot, get excited! Tell him how good he is, rub his ears, or play chase with him in the yard. If it makes your puppy happy, it will work as a reward. In this situation a simple 'good boy' will not do. While your puppy is learning, you want him to look forward to the reward, so you need to make it as rewarding as possible. After your Papillon has gone potty, you can allow him to engage in play, explore the yard, and let him do what he wants.

Crate Training

Crates can make a world of difference in house-training. Most dogs do not like to mess in the same area that they sleep, so an appropriately sized crate can discourage them from eliminating in the house while you're busy or away from home. Many dogs will eventually find comfort in the crate as well, giving them a safe place to go when they are uncomfortable.

Proper crate training will never be accomplished if you only place your Papillon in the crate when you leave the house. It's important to work on this skill during your time at home or your dog may think of the crate as a punishment that happens when you leave. This can lead to difficulties in house-training and separation anxiety. Place your dog in his crate for short periods of time while you clean up or do household chores. If he can see you during this time, he will likely feel more comfortable being in the crate. If you'd like, you can occasionally drop a few treats into the crate when he's being especially calm. A great time to work on crate training is after your dog has relieved himself outside and had playtime. He'll be tired and won't need a bathroom for some time, so this is an excellent opportunity to let him rest in the comfort of his crate. Never put your puppy in his crate if he hasn't gone outside recently. This may encourage him to make a mess in the crate and will interfere with house-training.

Size matters when properly crate training a dog. You want the crate to be big enough for the dog to stand and lie comfortably, but not so big that he feels comfortable relieving himself. You may need to buy a smaller crate for young puppies and upgrade as they grow. Some wire crates also have removable panels that allow you to adjust the size of the kennel as your puppy grows. Estimate how large your Papillon will be as an adult when you buy the crate and adjust the panel as needed until you're using the entire crate.

The type of crate you choose is not as important as the size. Crates or kennels are available in a wide variety of materials. You can choose crates made of plastic, metal, wire mesh, or wood. Some dogs prefer crates that are more closed off, or covered, because it makes them feel secure. Others like to be able to see the world around them while they rest. Decide which option your dog prefers and what types of crate are available within your budget. Wire crates are typically the least expensive and can be covered if your dog prefers.

Playpens and Doggy Doors

As your puppy grows and can go for longer periods of time between potty breaks, you can start giving him a bit more freedom. One way of achieving this is to set up a playpen. A playpen will allow your Papillon more space to play and rest. It would be wise to line the bottom of the pen with puppy pads in case he does have an accident. A playpen will still limit his access to the house, so he can't get in trouble, but will give him more room to move around in than the crate.

Another option to provide your Papillon is a doggy door. Doggy doors allow your dog the freedom to choose when he goes outside and can help prevent accidents indoors. Different types of doors are available, depending on your own preferences and the layout of your house. There are doors that install easily into sliding glass doors and which can be removed at any time. These can make the sliding door a bit difficult to use for people, so consider how much you use the door before going with this option. Other types of doors can be installed in the wall of your house. These types of door generally have two flaps to prevent a loss of heat in the winter. If you have other pets that you don't want to go outside or are worried about neighborhood pets or wild animals coming in the door, there are doggy doors that stay locked unless an animal is wearing a special tag on his collar. If you do purchase a doggy door, look for one with a size-appropriate flap. Papillons are petite dogs, and particularly small ones may struggle with going through doggy doors with big, heavy flaps.

Both options allow your Papillon to have more freedom than a crate when he's not being directly supervised. However, take time to consider whether your puppy is ready for that much freedom. More space inside means more space for messes. Playpens may not be as secure as a crate and your puppy may escape to cause trouble in the rest of the house.

Photo Courtesy of
Kody Kilcrease

The same concerns apply to Papillons with access to a doggy door. Papillons are small dogs, especially as puppies, so you need to be entirely sure of the security of your yard before allowing him to go out unsupervised. Wild animals or neighborhood pets are also a safety concern. If there is any possibility of another animal gaining access to your yard, reconsider putting in that doggy door.

CHAPTER 7
Socializing with People and Animals

"We never let our Papillons (puppies or adults) play with large dogs or prey dogs, they tend to think a Papillon is a bunny."

Sally Howard
Tiny T Papillons / K's Klassic Ponies

The Importance of Good Socialization

A Papillon who has been properly socialized is an excellent companion that can confidently accompany his owner anywhere. This means your dog can go to the vet, groomer, or pet sitter without unnecessary stress. He can accompany you on your errands, on vacation, and even to work if your employer allows it. A properly socialized dog is a pleasure to be around and will be welcomed anywhere dogs are allowed. Many businesses are happy to have well-behaved dogs visit them, even if they aren't typically dog-friendly.

Polite dogs are ambassadors not only for their breed, but their species as well, so socialization is an opportunity for positive representation as well. A Papillon who is insecure or aggressive in public, barking and snapping at other people or dogs, leaves a lasting impression on people, so the next time they see a Papillon, they may expect the same type of behavior. This may cause businesses to no longer allow dogs, or even give the breed a bad reputation. Although the breed is on the rise, Papillons are not an especially common breed, so socialization is essential in allowing them to develop the friendly, bubbly temperament they are known for.

Good socialization is also important to your Papillon's overall happiness and wellbeing. Your dog will be able to accompany you wherever you go and meet new friends without experiencing unhealthy amounts of stress. Socialization allows your dog to make more friends and have more opportunities to play. Not only is this good for your dog's mental health, but the physical activity involved in play will keep him fit. The physical and mental stimulation means your dog will be calmer and more

Photo Courtesy of Lisa Nawrocki

well-behaved at home. When out in public, he'll focus more on you and less on the environment, allowing you to focus more on training. Simply put, good socialization allows your dog to be the best dog he can be.

Proper socialization means exposing your dog to a variety of positive experiences with other animals and humans. Beware of any situation in which your Papillon may become overwhelmed. Even a single negative experience can leave a lasting mark on your dog's mind and it may take a significant amount of training to overcome. Dog parks may seem like a great place to socialize your dog, but they are one of the worst. Besides the obvious physical danger to a petite Papillon, other dog owners often pay little attention to their dogs' behavior and body language. Veterinary professionals see injuries resulting from dog park fights on a regular basis. Even if your dog isn't physically harmed, the high energy and emotions of a dog park can be overwhelming and could cause your Papillon to develop anxiety around other dogs. Instead, consider setting up play-dates with friends, family, or other dog owners in your community. Many owners are happy to give their dog a chance to play and socialize outside of the wild and unrestrained atmosphere of the dog park.

Photo Courtesy of Susanne Hudler

Behavior Around Other Dogs

Papillons typically get along well with other dogs of any size. Their happy, playful demeanor usually results in instant friendship. Occasionally, you may find your Papillon getting jealous of other dogs or being a bully. It's essential to put a stop to this behavior the instant you notice it. Papillons can easily develop what is known as "small dog syndrome." Small dogs are often allowed to get away with behaviors that would not be tolerated in a larger dog. Behaviors such as growling, bullying other dogs, or dominance-related behavior would be inappropriate and potentially dangerous in a big dog. These behaviors are often overlooked in smaller dogs because they aren't seen as a threat. However, if your Papillon displays any aggressive or dominant behavior, he may find himself in trouble, especially if he gets in a fight with a larger dog. Papillons may be small and cute, but they must be responsible citizens just like their larger counterparts.

Understanding your Papillon's body language and how he interacts with other dogs can prevent problems and possibly even save his life. When dogs greet each other in a friendly manner, they will approach each other with a relaxed posture and wagging tail. Their ears may be

Photo Courtesy of Middy Mentzer

perked up in interest, but not with intensity. They may sniff each other for a moment before engaging in play or going their separate ways. If either dog demonstrates a stiff posture with their head in the air and their ears back, this greeting may not go well. They may growl or bare their teeth as well. Dogs who display this tense body language may be wagging their tails, but this is not a friendly wag. Likewise, be cautious around dogs who show fearful postures. Fear can quickly turn into aggression with little provocation. Fearful dogs will cower and tuck their tail between their legs. They may lick their lips or show their teeth in submission. Some dogs will even urinate submissively when greeting other dogs. If either your Papillon or his friend display anything but relaxed, cheerful body language, be cautious and use your best judgment whether to continue the introduction.

Your body language can easily influence your Papillon's, so it's important that you remain relaxed and calm during any greeting or interaction with another dog. Avoid tensing your body or gripping the leash too tightly. Your dog can sense your tension and will believe that there is a reason to be worried. Most of the time, your Papillon will handle interactions with the friendly demeanor his breed is known for, so there's no need for you to be tense.

However, always keep a close eye on your Papillon while he interacts with other dogs. It takes only a moment for a fight to break out if you aren't watching for inappropriate body language. Just because your Papillon has good social skills doesn't mean every other dog does. Papillons are small dogs, and it doesn't take much of a fight to seriously injure or kill them. If you have doubts about another dog, stay on the safe side and avoid interacting with them.

Ways to Socialize Your Dog with Other Pets

Safely exposing your Papillon to a variety of different pets will make him a more confident dog overall. You'll have a self-assured companion who can accompany you anywhere, no matter what type of pets he may encounter. If you have no other pets at home, ask your friends or family if you can introduce your Papillon to their pets. Well-socialized Papillons can safely interact with a variety of animals, large and small, but it does take time and commitment to training. Many Papillons live comfortably on farms or with exotic pets, but this depends entirely on the individual dog's socialization and training. Some dogs need more time to adjust to different types of animals, while others adapt more quickly.

The most important aspect of socializing your dog with other pets is making sure he isn't overwhelmed by the experience. As with meeting other dogs, stay calm and keep an eye on everyone's body language. If your dog exhibits signs of anxiety, fear, or aggression, remove him from the situation immediately. Although they are small, overly enthusiastic Papillons can be intimidating to some animals, so watch the other pet's body language, too. Cats can be especially sensitive to energetic little dogs in their personal space and can react quickly and aggressively, so be prepared to intervene if necessary. Introductions can be a positive or negative socialization experience, depending on how they go, so slow introductions are best when socializing your dog with other pets.

When introducing your dog to other types of pets, it's best to keep him on a leash. Remember, Papillons are small enough that they can find themselves in big trouble in the blink of an eye. Some Papillons also have high prey drives and they may try to chase other animals. Depending on the type of animal you're introducing to your Papillon, it may be wise to have the other animal restrained as well to prevent any accidents. If the other animals, or your Papillon, are particularly territorial, try to introduce them on neutral ground if possible. This will prevent either animal from feeling the need to defend their territory and will set the tone for a positive experience.

Photo Courtesy of Sue Dempster

Never leave your Papillon unsupervised around other pets until you are sure that they have spent enough supervised time around each other to be trusted. Papillons are small enough that being scratched by a cat or stepped on by a larger animal can cause serious damage. This may mean several weeks or months of supervision before allowing the animals to be left alone together. In the case of larger animals, such as horses or cows, it may not be a good idea to ever allow them to be alone unsupervised.

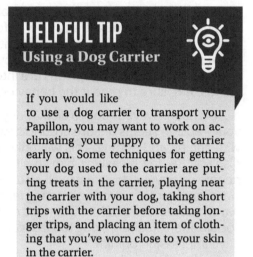

HELPFUL TIP

Using a Dog Carrier

If you would like to use a dog carrier to transport your Papillon, you may want to work on acclimating your puppy to the carrier early on. Some techniques for getting your dog used to the carrier are putting treats in the carrier, playing near the carrier with your dog, taking short trips with the carrier before taking longer trips, and placing an item of clothing that you've worn close to your skin in the carrier.

Properly Greeting New People

Papillons are typically confident little dogs who boldly approach strangers. They are usually happy to make new friends everywhere they go. However, some dogs may need a little help with introductions. Whether your dog is naturally bold or timid, proper greetings are key to a well-socialized Papillon.

Depending on your dog's past, he may be wary of certain types of people. Dogs who haven't been socialized around men, for instance, may be completely comfortable around most women, but could show fear or anxiety when in the presence of men. When socializing your dog, try to introduce him to as many different types of people as you can. The more people he meets, the more confident he will be when he accompanies you in public.

Allow your dog to approach new people on their own. Shoving your dog into the arms of a stranger can be overwhelming to an insecure dog and can result in fear-based aggression. Instead, have the person offer your Papillon a few of his favorite treats. Don't let them try to pet him right away if he's uncomfortable. Allow the Papillon time to realize that the stranger is not a threat. If your Papillon is more confident, he may try to jump on new people or lick them. Many people do not enjoy being greeted this way, so it's best to encourage your dog to greet strangers in a calm and polite manner. Having your dog on a leash when meeting people will keep him under your control and prevent him from jumping up. Encourage your dog to sit and wait for the person to pet him. Ask the person not to pet or talk to the dog until he's sitting calmly. It may take a few repetitions for an excitable puppy before he understands what is being asked of him, but Papillons are intelligent dogs and once he understands, he's sure to repeat the behavior.

Do not allow your dog to display any fearful or aggressive behavior. If your Papillon seems unsure around new people, do not comfort the dog with cooing and petting. This will only encourage the behavior. Instead, distract the dog by asking him to sit and offering treats. Having other people offer your dog treats will also encourage him to be friendlier toward strangers. If your dog is acting fearful or aggressive, make sure you haven't asked more of him than he's comfortable with at this stage in his socialization. Pushing a dog too fast can overwhelm him and leave a negative impression on him.

As always, encourage polite behavior with positive reinforcement. When your dog properly greets someone, praise him. If your dog is particularly timid around strangers, you may want to give the stranger a few treats to encourage your Papillon to approach. Once he realizes that strangers are a source of treats and affection, he'll be able to approach them more confidently.

Papillons and Children

Kids and Papillons can be perfect companions, but only if both the children and the dog are taught to interact responsibly. Small children can be too rambunctious for a tiny puppy and could scare or hurt him accidentally. Likewise, a frightened or injured Papillon may lash out at a child and bite them. With proper supervision and a little training, Papillons and children can become the best of friends. Just be prepared to invest some time into preparing them both for the responsibility of being in each other's company.

When preparing to introduce your Papillon to children, have a conversation with the kids and make sure they are responsible enough to interact with such a small dog. Young children, and especially toddlers, often treat dogs the way they treat their stuffed animals, not realizing they can hurt a real dog. This often results in the dog defending itself by biting the child. So, to prevent any injuries, it's important to talk to the children and explain how to properly interact with a dog. Explain to them that they must be gentle with the dog and discourage them from attempting to pick the dog up. If they are used to playing with larger dogs, it must be made clear that they can't roughhouse with a Papillon the way they would with a larger breed. Once you are sure that they understand, then you can introduce them to your new Papillon.

Go slowly when introducing your Papillon to children. Both kids and puppies are easily excited, and things can escalate quickly without intervention, so only allow them to interact when everyone can remain calm and under control. Be ready to correct inappropriate behavior and encourage gentle play. You may only be able to have the puppy and children together for a few minutes at a time at first, but you can slowly increase the amount of time as they get used to each other. Excited children can be loud and scary to a tiny Papillon, so it may take time and encouragement to get your Papillon comfortable in their presence. Use positive reinforcement and praise both the children and Papillon when they interact in a calm and gentle manner. If your Papillon is particularly hesitant about approaching the children, have them offer a few treats. Feeding the dog out of their hands, without attempting to touch him right away, will show him that children are friendly and nothing to be afraid of. With enough patience and encouragement, your Papillon and children will become the best of friends.

Do not leave your children unattended with your new Papillon under any circumstances. Accidents can happen quickly and can only be prevented with proper supervision. It's unlikely that either the dog or the children would want to hurt the other intentionally, but it's easy for an overly enthusiastic child to scare or accidentally injure such a delicate dog. To prevent anyone from getting injured or worse, it's best to keep an eye on everyone.

CHAPTER 8
Papillons and Your Other Pets

"Be watchful with all other pets when they first come home. Let them interact with your supervision. Usually they will take care of themselves, but problems can arise."

Nana Ridgeway
Nanken Papillons

Introducing Your New Puppy to Other Animals

When first introducing your Papillon to other animals, it's best to allow both the puppy and the other animal to view each other from a distance at first. As the animals become more comfortable with each other, you can allow them to get closer. If either animal shows signs of stress or anxiety, increase the distance and allow them to relax before attempting to approach the other animal again. If both the puppy and the other animal are comfortable, you can allow them to meet face to face and check each other out.

It's best to do initial introductions with both the Papillon and the other animal being restrained. Papillon puppies are quite delicate and can be easily hurt by an animal of any species. Likewise, an excitable puppy can be frightening to some animals and they may react out of fear. Restraining both animals will also allow you to quickly separate them if things don't go as planned.

As with any new situation, never leave your Papillon and another animal left unsupervised. Accidents can happen quickly and without warning, so to prevent any serious injuries or tragedies, keep an eye on them at all times. Even if the puppy and other animal are getting along well, supervision is still required in case they play a little too rough or manage to get themselves into trouble. Watch their body language for any signs of fear or stress and separate them if necessary.

Photo Courtesy of
Marte Pedersen

Pack Mentality

Dogs are social animals that typically have a well-structured hierarchy within their group. Dogs find comfort in that hierarchy and in the rules and limitations set in place by their leader. Dogs are natural followers but will take over as leaders if they are not provided with one. Some dogs are more dominant, while others are more submissive, so your dog's individual personality will determine how easy it is for her to accept her place within the pack. Whether you have several other pets, or just a Papillon, it's important to set clear boundaries and be the leader your dog needs you to be. A dog without limitations or rules can be unmanageable or even dangerous. Just because Papillons are small doesn't mean they get a pass on bad behavior.

Papillons, and other small breeds, are often allowed to get away with behaviors that are considered unacceptable in big dogs. This collection of behaviors is known as 'small dog syndrome' and is a result of small dogs being treated more like stuffed animals than the petite descen-

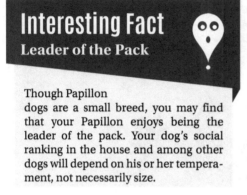

Interesting Fact
Leader of the Pack

Though Papillon dogs are a small breed, you may find that your Papillon enjoys being the leader of the pack. Your dog's social ranking in the house and among other dogs will depend on his or her temperament, not necessarily size.

dants of wolves. Just because a dog is tiny doesn't mean he doesn't need leadership. Symptoms of small dog syndrome includes jumping up on people, growling or snapping, hiding behind or being overly protective of their owner, and a reluctance or failure to obey commands. Dogs who behave this way will often refuse to move when asked or will display 'resource guarding' or aggression when humans or other dogs try to take their food or toys. Owners of small dogs often neglect to correct these behaviors because the dogs aren't as dangerous or unmanageable as their larger counterparts. Fortunately, this attitude is easily corrected with consistent leadership, training, and exercise. If your Papillon begins to display any of the behaviors associated with small dog syndrome, correct it immediately. If you are having trouble correcting your dog's behavior, contact a professional trainer as soon as possible.

In a natural pack setting, the pack leader is the first to eat, sleeps where he wants to, and never moves out of the way of other pack members. As the leader of your own pack, it's important to set your own boundaries and enforce them accordingly. Never hit, kick, or yell at your dog as a correction. Your dog won't understand the correction and will only learn to be afraid of you. Natural pack leaders correct with small nips, nudges, and growls. You can imitate this behavior by teaching your dog the word 'no' and using the body language of a leader. At feeding time, ask your dog to sit, and wait patiently while you set her bowl down. Don't let her eat the moment the bowl hits the floor. Instead, have her wait a few seconds before allowing her to eat. With practice, you can increase the time and have your dog wait as long as you'd like before eating. When going through doorways, you must always be first to enter. A dog who rushes past you out the door does not know her place in the pack. Again, have your Papillon sit and wait patiently until you release her, allowing her to walk through the doorway. If your dog is sitting in your favorite chair, you can tell her to leave. Your dog's feelings won't be hurt if she has to find another place to sleep, and you will maintain your place in the hierarchy of the household. In the wild, dogs depend on this social order, and it should be no different in your home. It's crucial to remain calm, assertive, and consistent in your leadership in order to maintain a well-behaved, stable pack.

Fighting and Bad Behavior

"Papillons like to pick on other types of dogs or younger/smaller Papillons. They will pick on that particular dog until it begins to cry out or bark back, and then the treatment gets even worse. If you have several Paps, it can become a gang fight. As with any type of dog, it is the rule of the pack. Always be aware of what is going on with your dog. If you have more than one, make sure that they all get along."

Amanda Vidrine

Earth Angels' – Chihuahuas and Papillons

Photo Courtesy of
Talia Fuchs

Photo Courtesy of
Gill Breen

If your Papillon begins to display aggressive behavior, you need to act immediately. It may start out as nothing more than a growl or pushing another dog away from their food bowl, but if this behavior is allowed to happen it may escalate into more serious and more dangerous behavior. Even a fight with another small dog can result in serious injuries, and if your Papillon picks a fight with a bigger dog it may end in life-threatening wounds. Your Papillon's behavior needs to be corrected at the first hint of aggression to prevent escalation. Do not allow your Papillon to bully other dogs or display resource- guarding behavior. Dogs should be allowed to have their own personal boundaries, of course, but within reason. Correct your Papillon's aggressive behavior by clapping loudly or stomping to distract her. If possible, call her away from the situation and redirect her attention by asking her to perform simple tasks such as "sit" or "down." Forcing her to focus on you instead of the other dog can diffuse the situation and prevent a fight.

Correcting aggressive behavior and diffusing stressful situations is the first step to managing aggressive behavior, but to prevent aggression from occurring in the first place you need to determine why your dog may be starting fights. Think about the situations in which your dog has become aggressive and consider what each of those incidents may have in common. If you can figure out what is triggering your dog's aggression, you can either remove the stressor or better manage it. If your dogs consistently fight over chew toys, it may be time to remove chew toys from the household, or to separate the dogs while they chew. This type of resource-guarding behavior may also occur over a favorite sleeping spot, room, or human. If your older dog starts a fight every time the younger one tries to play with him, or plays too rough, she may be experiencing pain from arthritis that is aggravated when the younger dog jumps on her. If you can figure out what is causing your dogs to fight, you can manage your dogs' behavior more easily.

If your dogs' aggressive behavior escalates into an actual fight, do not break up the fight by grabbing one or both dogs. This is likely to result in you getting bitten, and possibly seriously injured. There are other options you can use to break up the fight, but be aware you may need to try a few before the fight actually stops. Try making loud noises to distract the dogs. This is one time where it is appropriate to yell at your dogs. Yell, clap loudly, stomp, or tap on a metal bowl if you have one nearby. Often, this is enough to redirect the dogs' attention and stop the fight. Spraying the dogs with water is another option. If you have a spray bottle or hose nearby, don't be afraid to soak the dogs. This will not hurt them but will probably be surprising enough to put a stop to their behavior. If you must intervene physically, decide which dog is the aggressor and which dog is defending himself. Grab the more aggressive dog by the back legs and pull her away from the other dog. It's important to do this quickly enough that she can't turn around and bite you. Once you have the dogs pulled apart, quickly restrain them or separate them to prevent another fight.

Aggression can be a dangerous and difficult behavior to deal with. However, it's important to recognize when the situation has gotten out of your control. If you don't think you are able to manage your dogs' behavior anymore, contact a professional trainer or behaviorist immediately. The sooner you can take the steps to manage the aggression, the less it will be allowed to escalate. Dog fights can end in tragedy, so seek help as soon as possible.

Raising Multiple Puppies From the Same Litter

Adopting two or more Papillons from the same litter can seem like a great idea, especially if you have no other animals. Your puppies will likely be more confident coming into your household with their siblings, with whom they've already developed a bond. You'll never have to worry about leaving them home alone, and they'll always have a playmate. Additionally, you'll know that the dogs already get along before bringing them home. This reduces the amount of time involved with introducing a new dog into your household. Having more puppies will also reduce the amount of time you spend keeping your dogs busy because they'll have someone to play with while you do household chores or run errands.

There are, however, drawbacks to having multiple puppies out the same litter. More puppies mean you'll have more trouble and more mess. You'll be supervising and training multiple dogs, so time management is especially important. It might be great that your dogs have a close bond, but this can also be a problem if you ever need to separate them, even temporarily. If one dog needs to go to the vet, for instance, you may find that the other will exhibit signs of extreme stress and anxiety over being separated. Dogs who have been raised with siblings can be extremely insecure and fearful when separated from their littermates. If your dogs develop bad habits or even fearful or aggressive behavior, it can be significantly more difficult to break those habits when working with multiple dogs.

If you do choose to adopt two or more puppies from the same litter, carefully consider how much time you can commit to your dogs. If you work eight hours a day and have any hobbies, you may find that keeping up with one dog is difficult as is. House-training can be especially difficult when you need to keep an eye on multiple puppies running around the house. When training your Papillons, it may be wise to take them each out on their own to work on their training. This allows the dogs to get used to being separated temporarily while also being out on their own. It's important to socialize the dogs separately to help build their confidence in encountering new situations. Likewise, you need to socialize and train them together to be sure that you can properly manage the group when taking them on walks or to the vet or groomer. If you're in doubt as to whether you can handle training multiple Papillons at a time, consider adopting one at first and when you have the first dog trained and socialized well enough, you can consider adopting another.

Options If Your Pets Don't Get Along

Some pets may simply need more time to adjust to living together. Don't rush the introductions, and certainly don't rush any serious decisions regarding your current pets and new Papillon. It may take weeks, or even months, before your pets can be trusted together. If you've had a pet for a long time before bringing

Photo Courtesy of Senga Arbuckle

your Papillon home, he may just need more time before he fully adjusts to living with another pet. Sharing space and affection can be difficult for some pets, especially if they've been an only pet for most of their lives. The more time you are willing to commit to training and socialization, the more quickly and smooth the introductions will be, so be prepared to spend a significant amount of time working to familiarize your pets with each other.

The thought of giving up a beloved pet can be distressing, so if you aren't willing to consider that option, you'll need to work on keeping the animals separated. Determine whether you are willing to put in the time and energy it will take to manage your pets for their entire lifetime. Making sure that pets have no interaction with each other but still receive equal amounts of attention and exercise can be exhausting, especially if it must be done for the lifetime of the animals. You will need to provide each pet with a safe, comfortable place to stay out of reach of the other pets. Keeping pets separated for their entire lives can be stressful, exhausting, and time-consuming, so carefully consider whether you are able to provide this level of your care for your pets and whether it's truly the best situation for them.

If you've exhausted your options in managing your pets' behavior and can't see yourself keeping them separated for the next 10-15 years, it may be time to consider finding another home for one of your pets. Some pets may do better in a single-pet home, while others may simply need a different environment to thrive. It may be a heartbreaking decision to make, but it's your responsibility as a pet owner to make the right decisions regarding the welfare of your pets.

CHAPTER 9
Physical and Mental Exercise

Exercise Requirements

You may look at petite Papillons and assume that their need for exercise would be minimal. According to Amanda Vidrine of Earth Angels Papillons, "Papillons may be a toy breed, but that doesn't mean they don't need a lot of physical exercise." Papillons are energetic, active little dogs that thrive on physical and mental activities. Without enough physical exercise, they may become overweight and develop a variety of weight-related health problems. A Papillon who is not regularly challenged with mental stimulation may become destructive or develop behavioral problems. A tired dog will also be easier to manage in the house and out in public.

Depending on your Papillon's age, energy level, and overall health, your dog will need between 30 minutes and two hours of physical activity every day. This may include walking, hiking, playing, or training sessions. For young puppies, it's best to give them short periods of playtime or walking several times per day. Limit each session to five to 15 minutes every few hours. Older dogs will have more stamina and will be able to handle longer sessions. Ideally, your adult dog will have one exercise session in the morning and one in the evening. If you work long hours, your dog will rest easier and wait more patiently for your return if you exercise him before you leave. A tired dog is more likely to nap quietly throughout the day instead of finding something to do and getting into trouble.

FUN FACT
Fitness Pal

Health.com ranked Papillons among the top 15 dog breeds for active people due to their high energy and agility. Though Papillons may not be ideal distance runners, their energetic nature can help keep you motivated and moving while walking and playing together.

Mental exercise is just as important as physical exercise, especially with a breed as intelligent as the Papillon. Engaging your dog in stimulating training sessions and providing him with mental challenges will stave off boredom and behavioral problems. Papillons are excellent problem-solvers and eager learners, so don't

be afraid to challenge them. Mental challenges are also great for senior dogs or those with physical limitations. Mental exercise will wear your dog out quickly, so training sessions should last no longer than 15 minutes. You can repeat these sessions throughout the day to keep your dog focused and using his brain. Young puppies may not be able to focus for 15 minutes at a time, so they may need sessions as short as three to five minutes. In the long run, trying new dog sports, challenging your Papillon to work for his food, and keeping him busy while you're away will result in a happier, healthier, and more well-behaved dog.

Different Types of Exercise to Try

Papillons love any activity that involves spending time with their owners, so consider trying out a few different sports to see what you and your Papillon will excel in. Dog sports are an excellent way to keep your dog fit, but they are also an excellent way to keep your dog stimulated mentally. Cherish Dewitt of Playtyme Papillons says, "Typically, Papillons need something more to exercise the mind. This is where performance events can be very helpful. [In] agility, they are the leaders of the smaller heights. Obedience, they excel at. They can even be found herding sheep, lure coursing, dock diving, freestyle dancing, and more." Training and competing in dog sports is also an excellent way to strengthen the bond between you and your dog.

Photo Courtesy of Helen Parker

Obedience is one of the oldest competitive dog sports. Handlers and their dogs must walk or jog through the course and perform a variety of tasks including sitting, heeling, retrieving, and staying. There are different levels with different expectations for the dogs. Lower levels are done on-leash with only the most basic of tasks. Higher levels are done off-leash and involve more difficult tasks such as jumping over obstacles to retrieve dumbbells. If classic obedience competitions aren't for you, consider competing in rally obedience. Rally obedience is a faster-paced version where handlers and dogs navigate a course of 10-20 tasks. Each task is marked by a sign with instructions, and each team is timed as it goes through the course. Dog and handler must work as a team to quickly and accurate navigate the course.

Agility is an exciting event where a handler instructs their dog to race around a course jumping over obstacles, running through tunnels, weaving through poles, and more. The competitors are divided into groups based on their height and each lap is timed. The fastest dog in each height category wins.

Flyball is another sport in which Papillons excel. This high-energy relay race is perfect for fast dogs who love to play fetch. Dogs compete on teams and they must race, one at a time, over a series of hurdles before pouncing on a box that launches a tennis ball into their mouth. They must then race back to the start where the next dog is awaiting their turn. Speed and agility are essential to this fast-paced, exciting sport.

If your Papillon displays a high prey drive, he may enjoy competing in barn hunt competitions. This sport is not as well known as obedience or agility but is on the rise. Handlers release their dogs in an enclosed area filled with stacked haybales. Dogs must search the haybales for the scent of rodents. The goal is for the dogs to locate the rats, which are kept safely in a cage, out of the dogs' reach.

The sport of scent work showcases your Papillon's incredible sense of smell. Scent work doesn't require a high level of physical fitness so it's a great sport for older or disabled dogs, or those who prefer a lower- energy sport. Based on the work of professional detection dogs, the handler and dog must locate cotton swabs dipped in the essential oils of anise, birch, clove, and cypress. Once found, the dog must signal to the handler, who then alerts the judge.

If you're interested in trying out a specific sport, contact your local club and see if you can watch a training session or competition. Checking out the sport and talking with the other competitors will help you to decide if you want to try it with your Papillon. Some dogs prefer certain sports over others, so be willing to try a few to see which you both like best.

Photo Courtesy of Susan Appelgren

Importance of Mental Exercise

With an intelligent breed such as the Papillon, mental exercise is essential to the health and well-being of your dog. Dogs who don't receive enough mental stimulation may find other ways to entertain themselves, usually in a way that gets them into trouble. They may begin to destroy toys, furniture, or your favorite slippers. Behavior problems such as excessive barking may also develop. You may find that you can walk your Papillon all day and he never seems to get tired, but after a 15-minute obedience, session he's ready for a nap. Mental stimulation can wear out a puppy much faster than long walks or play sessions, resulting in a calmer, more focused dog.

Mental exercise is especially important with dogs with physical limitations. If dogs are exercised too much at a young age they can develop serious bone and joint problems later in life, so mental stimulation is especially important for growing puppies. As dogs age, they may develop arthritis or other problems that limit their physical abilities, so providing them with mental stimulation will prevent boredom and increase their quality of life. Sports such as scent work or challenging toys are great for dogs who can't go for long walks or compete in more demanding sports. Old dogs can always learn new tricks, so try teaching your senior Papillon to shake paws or speak. Short training sessions are a great way to keep your dog's mind sharp as he ages.

Mental stimulation can be exhausting, so keep your training sessions short and focused on one or two tasks at a time. If you're teaching your dog a new trick, focus on that trick for to 5-15 minutes and then let him play or rest. If you try to pack your session full of different tasks, he may become tired or frustrated and lose interest. Training sessions are only of value when the dog is interested, so quit before he becomes distracted. If you notice he becomes less responsive after 10 minutes of training, stop the session at eight minutes and try again later. After a brief rest or play session, your dog will be ready to try again later.

Tips for Keeping Your Papillon Occupied

An unoccupied Papillon is likely a Papillon getting into trouble. Keeping such an intelligent breed busy can be quite a challenge, but there are many options for entertaining your dog while you're away from the house or simply want to get some work done at home. Since most dogs are at least somewhat food motivated, hiding food in various types of toys is one of the best ways to keep your Papillon occupied. Some owners even hide bits of food around the house to give their dogs a scavenger-hunt type of activity. Frozen treats are also a great way to keep your dog busy, especially if he's figured out how to quickly remove food from

Photo Courtesy of
Aisling Murtagh

Photo Courtesy of Pat Meehan

his toys or puzzles. Even though these activities are a great way to exercise your dog's mind, they can spell trouble for his body if you don't factor the calories of the hidden treats into his daily diet. If you're worried about your Papillon's waistline, you can serve a portion of his meals in the toys or games, or even his entire meal if you want to spread it out over a few different toys or sessions throughout the day.

Puzzle toys are a great option for your Papillon to practice his problem-solving skills and to keep him out of trouble. These wooden or plastic toys usually have flaps, knobs, cups, or sliding doors that your dog must maneuver to reach the tasty treats hidden inside. You can hide treats in the puzzle and let him work for it while you're gone or doing household chores. Be aware that a Papillon's intelligence will help him figure out the puzzle toy quickly, so many owners opt to have several different toys and rotate them to give their dogs a new challenge each day. Some companies even offer puzzles with varying levels of difficulty, so you can start with easy puzzles and progress to more challenging puzzles as your dog learns how to work them.

Rubber chew toys, such as Kongs, are an excellent way to challenge your dog and keep him out of trouble. These types of toy typically have a narrow, hollow center where you can stuff food or treats. They are made of a tough rubber material and come in a variety of sizes and densities to suit your individual dog's needs. You can use any kind of food or combination of food including kibble, canned food, vegetables, or specially made treat pastes. Some dogs quickly learn to hold the toy with their paw while they lick out the food, so if your Papillon empties the toy in record time you can try freezing it for more of a challenge. This is also a great way to keep your dog cool in the summer heat. Many owners buy a few of these toys, fill them all at once, and keep them stored in the freezer so they can easily serve them at any time.

Snuffle mats are gaining popularity with owners of food-driven dogs. They are flat mats made from an easy-to-clean material such as fleece and feature long strips of fabric that resemble a shag rug. You can buy them in many pet stores or make your own. They are easy and inexpensive to make, require just a few materials, and instructions can easily be found on the internet. Take a small number of treats or pieces of kibble and sprinkle throughout the mat. You may need to fluff up the strips of fabric to properly hide the treats. These mats encourage your dog to utilize his superior sense of smell to find the food hidden within the fabric. This is an activity any dog can do, including older or physically challenged dogs. Even young puppies enjoy the challenge of foraging for their food.

CHAPTER 10
Training Your Papillon

"They learn very quickly, so be sure you are teaching them the lessons and manners you will want them to have for all of their lives. Decide before you bring the puppy home if it's going to be allowed on the furniture, or are certain rooms off limits, where they will be fed and when, where they are going to sleep, if jumping on people will be allowed, front door manners, etc. The new puppy will learn bad habits if you don't teach them good habits right away. Do not allow bad behavior to go unaddressed just because the puppy is so cute."

Cynthia Springer
Rocyn Papillons

Clear Expectations

It's important to have clear expectations of both yourself and your Papillon during training sessions. Remember, progress can only be made with clear and consistent communication. It's your responsibility to make sure you're setting your dog up for success. If you only train once a week, and you aren't clear about what you're asking of your dog, you're going to walk away from your training sessions disappointed and frustrated. Your dog will also be more likely to lose focus or motivation in your next session. Setting small goals for each session and planning out how you'll accomplish those goals will help you be more successful in your training.

Do not ask more of your dog than he is capable of at the present stage of his training. For example, if your dog is able to respond to your commands inside your house, but his responses are inconsistent in your backyard, do not take him to the dog park and expect him to listen to you. Training must be done in small steps to avoid overwhelming your dog and leaving him with a bad experience. Begin training your dog in an environment with few distractions and work your way up to places with more commotion when he's ready. If you know your dog is reactive in certain situations, you must avoid those

Photo Courtesy of April LaCroix

situations until he's ready. You can only expect your dog to behave in situations you've prepared him for.

Always end your training sessions on a positive note. Once you start working with your dog you'll begin to notice when he starts getting tired and losing focus. Working past this point will only result in frustration and will set your next training session up for failure. Once your dog performs the correct behavior a few times, it may be time to quit. You can always come back and practice more at a later time. If your dog seems to be struggling with a certain task, try asking him to do something easier that he already knows. This way, you can reward him for correctly performing that behavior, end your session on a positive note, and try working on the original task later.

Operant Conditioning Basics

Operant conditioning is a type of learning based on the reward or punishment resulting from a particular behavior. This method was originally studied and promoted by American psychologist and behaviorist B.F. Skinner. Skinner believed that humans and animals were too complex to learn by classical conditioning alone. He theorized that behaviors that were followed by positive experiences were more likely to be repeated than those followed by negative experiences. Skinner identified three types of environmental responses that can shape behavior. Neutral operants are environmental responses that do not increase or decrease the likelihood of the behavior being repeated in the future. Reinforcers, which can be either positive or negative, increase the probability of the behavior being performed. Punishment discourages the behavior and decreases the likelihood of it being repeated in the future.

Positive reinforcement is one of the most effective and popular training methods for dogs. In dog training, positive reinforcement is most often seen in the form of treats and praise. If the dog has a positive experience after performing a specific behavior, this encourages him to repeat the behavior in the future. Nicholas Forbes of DreamPaps Papillon says, "Papillons are extremely intelligent and easy to train when using positive reinforcement." Most dogs are motivated by either food or praise, so they usually learn quickly when rewarded in this manner. Unfortunately, positive reinforcement can also result in bad behaviors. For instance, if your Papillon bolts out the door and is rewarded with the positive experience of being able to run around the neighborhood off-leash, he's more likely to repeat the behavior. Bad habits can develop quickly if you aren't careful about managing your dog's behavior and the environmental responses to his actions.

Negative reinforcement encourages the repetition of a specific behavior by removing an unpleasant stimulus from the dog's environment. This is not to be confused with a punishment. An example might come from leash training your dog. When you instruct your puppy to follow you on-leash, you may put a small amount of pressure on the leash. This creates an unpleasant pressure on the dog's body, either from a collar or a harness. Once the puppy moves forward, the pressure is released. Soon, the dog learns that moving with the leash rather than against it will prevent pressure from the collar or harness and he will be more likely to repeat this behavior in the future.

Punishments are negative experiences that decrease the probability of a behavior being repeated in the future. For example, if your Papillon urinates on the floor and you react with a yell, clap, or stomp every time he does this, he will eventually connect the sudden, unpleasant sound with his own behavior. This will discourage him from repeating this behavior in the future. However, if a punishment is too harsh, this may leave a lasting impression on the dog, resulting in fearful or aggressive behavior. Punishments should be used as little as possible and should never come in the form of hitting, kicking, or screaming at your dog. A simple clap, stomp, yelp, or even a quick spray of water is usually enough to discourage aggressive or destructive behavior.

Primary Reinforcements – Food, Toys, Playtime

Primary reinforcements are rewards that are biological in nature. This includes food, water, and pleasure. For dogs, this usually means treats, toys, and playtime. Dogs naturally find food and fun to be rewarding, and they will quickly learn to repeat behaviors that are followed by primary reinforcements. Toys and playtime also work as primary reinforcements because they imitate the natural behavior dogs use to chase and catch their prey. The thrill of the chase brings pleasure to dogs, so it's possible to use their natural prey drive as a primary reinforcement to encourage desired behaviors.

Photo Courtesy of Matt Glaser

Food is probably the best motivator for any dog. Biologically, they need it, but more

importantly, it makes them happy. As with people, individual dogs prefer certain foods over others, so what motivates one dog may not interest another. Foods that an individual dog prefers over all others are considered high-value. Many trainers reserve these high-value foods just for training sessions to encourage their dogs to work hard for their favorite foods. Some dogs may be motivated even by their daily kibble, in which case a portion of their daily meals can be used during training.

Some dogs may also be highly motivated by their favorite toy or game. Dogs with especially high prey drives will be more interested in being rewarded with toys than those with low prey drives. The key to reinforcing a behavior with the use of a toy or playtime is to make it exciting for a dog. Tug toys or toys that can be thrown are ideal. The key is to allow the dog to chase or go after the toy before being rewarded with a game of tug-of-war or fetch. It's natural for dogs to enjoy chasing their prey down and this type of play imitates that natural behavior, which is why it works as a primary reinforcement. Some dogs do not automatically make the connection between toys and prey, so food may be a better motivator for them. Find what motivates your dog and use it to your advantage.

Secondary Reinforcements – Attention, Praise, Clickers

Secondary reinforcements are rewards that are associated with primary reinforcements through experience. Dogs do not automatically know what "good dog" means, nor do they care about the sound of a clicker until they begin to associate these rewards with primary reinforcements. Secondary reinforcements can be used as rewards in training, but they must be taught before they have any value to a dog. Initially, you will need to use primary reinforcements, such as food or toys, to teach your dog to associate those rewards with secondary reinforcements. You will need to focus entirely on this connection before moving on to teaching your dog other commands.

Attention and praise work well as rewards, but some dogs do not value it as much as food or play. To teach your dog the value of praise, you need to come up with a word that he will recognize as a marker for good behavior. Use classical conditioning to teach him the value of words by saying "good" or "yes" while simultaneously giving him a treat when you reward good behavior. Eventually, you can start using the marker words and hesitating for a moment before giving him the food or toy. This will strengthen the value of this secondary reinforcement and allow you to work towards using more marker words and less food in future training sessions.

Clickers work in the same way that marker words do. This sound signals to the dog that he's performed the correct behavior, but it must be taught before the dog understands this concept. Begin teaching the dog by pressing the clicker as you give him a treat. After a few repetitions, you can try clicking first, then giving the treat. As your dog progresses with his training, you'll eventually be able to press the clicker to reward him for performing the correct behavior regardless of whether you have any treats on you.

When using secondary reinforcements in your training, you can eventually use them without primary reinforcements. However, over time, your dog's understanding of this connection may weaken and you may need to frequently go back to using treats and toys as a reward to maintain the value of attention, marker words, and sounds.

Negative Reinforcement

It may be difficult at first to understand the difference between negative reinforcement and punishment, but they are different concepts that can be used to encourage or discourage certain behaviors in your dog. When a dog performs an undesired behavior such as inappropriate barking and his behavior elicits a consequence such as a loud clap or stomp from you, this is a punishment. The behavior is followed by an unpleasant experience for the dog and discourages him from repeating this specific behavior in the future. A negative reinforcement is different in that respect. Negative reinforcements, when used correctly, will encourage the dog to repeat a certain behavior with the removal of an unpleasant stimulus or pressure when the dog performs the correct task.

An example of negative reinforcement may be found when teaching your dog to sit. You may ask your dog to sit and, as you give the command, you put your hand on his rear and gently press down to encourage him to sit. When he sits, this pressure is released. The dog will even-

tually learn that the only way to escape this pressure is to sit, which will encourage him to perform the behavior more frequently when given this command in the future.

You must be careful when using negative reinforcement in training your Papillon. If used incorrectly, your dog may not understand what you're asking of him and he may develop fearful or aversive behaviors during training sessions. Negative reinforcement is best used in combination with positive reinforcement. When you ask your dog to sit, it's fine to put pressure on his rear to encourage him to sit, but once he does so, remove the pressure from your hand and reward him with a primary or secondary reinforcement.

Hiring a Trainer & Attending Classes

Many dog owners are quite successful in training their dogs without the help of professionals. However, everyone makes mistakes, even if they've been lifelong dog owners. This doesn't mean you're a bad trainer, it just means it may take longer for you to reach the same point as someone who has been working with a professional. Professional trainers are experts in dog behavior and may be able to recognize and prevent problems before you are even aware of them. You'll be able to progress quicker and have any questions answered immediately. If you're planning on competing in dog sports, you'll need the guidance of a trainer to reach your dog's performance potential.

Most trainers offer their services in either private or group lessons. Both types of lessons have their advantages, so if you're considering working with a professional, decide what works best for you and your dog. In private lessons, you'll have the full attention of your trainer. This means you'll be able to make progress quickly and ask questions as you go. Private lessons are ideal for dogs with behavioral problems. If your dog exhibits aggression or fear around strange people or dogs, private lessons may be the best way to get help. Although you may not have the trainer's full attention in group lessons, you can still make considerable progress in your training in a group setting. Group sessions are usually cheaper than private lessons and are a great way to socialize your dog and practice working in an environment full of distractions. The more your dog can focus on you in a bustling group class, the more he'll be able to focus on your when confronted with strangers and their dogs in public.

If you are having any difficulties in your training, or you are struggling with getting your dog's behavior under control, it's important to recognize when you need help. The sooner you can seek help, the sooner your problems can be solved. This can prevent aggressive or fearful behavior from escalating into a potentially dangerous situation. Remember, professional trainers are there to help you and they won't judge or criticize your situation. They've likely encountered similar situations plenty of times in the past and are ready and willing to help you improve the relationship between you and your dog. There's no shame in asking for help, and you'll make improvements much more quickly than you would if you tried to tackle the situation yourself.

Owner Behavior

The most important aspect of dog training is holding yourself accountable for your own actions and behavior. If you aren't dedicated to your dog's training, your dog will recognize this. With consistency and enthusiasm, you and your Papillon will develop an unbreakable bond during your training sessions.

If you run into problems during your training, take some time to reflect on potential causes. Often, these difficulties are a result of miscom-

Photo Courtesy of Aisling Murtagh

munication or misunderstanding based on the owner's behavior. Dog training is a learning process for both owner and dog, and it's not uncommon to run into problems. However, you must be willing to look at your own behavior and be responsible for your own actions. The willingness to examine yourself and improve your own behavior will only make you a better trainer and will strengthen the relationship between you and your Papillon.

Sometimes you may not recognize problems in your own actions or behavior, so it may be helpful to have a friend or even a professional trainer with you during your training sessions. Having a second set of eyes on the situation may help you recognize behaviors you weren't even aware of. If you have friends or family that are dog owners, see if they are willing to discuss your situation or even take a look for themselves. Better yet, talk to a trainer or behaviorist and they will be able to help you with any problems you may be having. Remember, there's no shame in asking for help when you need it

CHAPTER 11
Basic Commands

Benefits of Proper Training

Photo Courtesy of Kelsey Corn

One of the most important benefits to training your Papillon is the mental stimulation it provides. Working with your dog in sessions as short as 5-10 minutes not only strengthens your bond, but it provides your dog the opportunity to exercise his brain. A dog who has had both his mind and body properly exercised will be calmer and more well-behaved. This, in turn, will allow him to focus more on you so you can continue teaching him.

Proper training will result in a Papillon who is a pleasure to be around. You can confidently take him anywhere you go, whether it's a cross-country road trip or simply on a walk around the neighborhood. If you've put the necessary time and dedication into your dog's training, you will be able to trust his reactions to new situations and he will be able to confidently handle whatever situation you may encounter. This will make socializing easier as well, because a well-trained dog will be better behaved around new people and other animals. Proper training is essential to a well-rounded, happy dog.

Different Training Methods

There are many different training methods to choose from, and every trainer likely does things a little differently, so you need to find what works best for you and your dog. For some, a training regimen of strictly positive reinforcement gets the best results. For others, they may need a combination of positive and negative reinforcement. If you choose to use a clicker in your training,

FUN FACT
World Record Holder

Konjo, a half Papillon dog from California, holds the record for running the fastest five meters on his front paws. Beating the previous record of 7.76 seconds, held by a dog named Jiff, Konjo ran the five meters in 2.39 seconds on December 22, 2014, in Tustin, California.

that is your choice to make. There may be some trial and error in finding the right method for you, so don't be afraid to try a few options before you settle on one. As always, if you seem to be struggling, reach out to a professional trainer and they may have the answer you were looking for.

Basic Commands

The sky is the limit in terms of things you can teach your Papillon. Sally Howard of Tiny T Papillons says, "Papillons are very smart and so are easy to train." However, there are a few basic commands that are crucial to your Papillon's education. Whether you are raising a future show-ring star or simply a cuddly companion, he needs to know how to sit, stay, lie down, and come. To maintain a balanced relationship, you must also teach him to get off furniture or give up a toy or chew when you ask. Loose leash walking will also make your life and his much easier.

Sit

The sit command is usually one the first commands taught to puppies because it's a relatively simple task and most puppies pick up on it quickly. It's a useful skill for any dog to learn because it puts the dog in a position where he can more easily look up at you to wait for further instructions. Combining the sit command with a 'stay' or 'wait' can help your dog learn patience when walking through doors, waiting for dinner, or spending time with you at the park or a café.

To teach your Papillon to sit, you can use a combination of positive and negative reinforcement, or positive reinforcement only. To use positive reinforcement, hold a treat in front of your dog's face to get his attention. Once he's focused on you, give the 'sit' command and raise the treat slightly above his head and out of reach, but not so high that he feels the need to jump up to get it. As you move the treat, he should sit so that he can reach the treat. You have two different options for negative reinforcement. Your first option is to place a hand on his hips, just in front of his tail, and put gentle pressure on him to further encourage him to sit. If you'd prefer to use a leash, or your dog has a habit of backing up when you ask him to sit, you can put gentle upward pressure on his leash to encourage him to look up to the treat. As soon as your Papillon sits, release the pressure, give him the treat, and praise him or press your clicker.

Stay

Stay is an excellent command to teach your dog patience and self-control. A stay can be performed while sitting, lying down, or standing. A dog with a solid stay should be able to wait patiently for you while you run into the coffee shop or while you prepare their dinner. As your Papillon progresses in his training, you'll be able to ask him to stay for longer periods of time and introduce more distractions. You can try rolling his favorite ball past him or dropping a few treats out of reach. Some obedience trainers differentiate between the 'stay' and 'wait' commands. 'Stay'

Photo Courtesy of Judith Sattler

is used for long periods of time and the dog is only released when the handler is standing next to him. For instance, if you ask your dog to wait outside a café while you order your coffee, you may choose to put him in a stay. 'Wait' is used for shorter periods and the dog may be released from a distance. You may use this command when asking your dog to wait while you set his dinner bowl down or as you practice your recall command from a distance. If you plan on competing in dog sports, this may also be a command that your dog is required to know.

Stay is a simple command to teach as you are just asking

your dog to continue the previous command. First, ask your dog to sit, lie down, or stand. Give him the command 'stay' and wait a few seconds. If he stays, reward him and praise him. If he doesn't stay, calmly start from the beginning and try again. As he learns what you're asking of him, you can increase the amount of time you ask him to stay and you can try taking a step or two away from him. Eventually, you can work up to giving him the command and leaving the room.

Lie Down

Once you've taught your Papillon how to sit, you can easily teach him to lie down. Teaching your dog this command is useful in many situations, such as for the vet or in the car. It also gives you another position to practice stays in. If you plan on teaching your Papillon any tricks, lying down can be the first step in teaching him to roll over or crawl. If you plan to compete in agility or obedience with your dog, this command may also be required in competition.

To teach your Papillon to lie down, first ask him to sit. Once he's sitting in front of you, give the command 'lie down' or 'down' and hold a treat in front of his nose to lure him down to the ground. Most dogs will follow the treat into a down position without standing up. However, if your dog is young and excitable, or has a high food drive, it may take a few repetitions for him to understand what you're asking. If he stands up, simply ask him to sit and start again from the beginning. Some dogs will also try to crouch without fully lying on the ground, so be sure to only reward him when he lies all the way down. Once he reaches the correct position, give him the treat and use the secondary reinforcement of your choice.

Come

Photo Courtesy of Salena Morrill

The 'come' command, or recall, is one of the most important commands you can teach your dog. This command is essential to your dog's training and may even save his life someday. Even if you don't intend to have your dog off-leash much, a solid recall is still important in case of emergencies. This command can be taught more easily with two handlers, so if you have a friend or family that can help, you may find your dog learns this command more easily. The recall is required in obedience competitions but is also useful in nearly every other dog sport that requires off-leash work, so it's a valuable skill to teach your dog if you plan on competing with him.

Start training your Papillon to come in an enclosed area, such as your yard or inside your house. As your practice your dog's recall, you can also find extra-long leashes at your local pet store or favorite online retailer. Using these leashes will allow you to practice in open spaces without risking your dog's safety. Ask your helper to hold onto your dog while you wait a short distance away with plenty of treats. As you give your dog the 'come' command, it's okay to act excited. Your excited tone of voice will encourage your Papillon to come to you, rather than wander about the yard or room. It may be helpful to have your helper hold onto your dog for a moment while you excitedly call your dog. Not being able to run to you immediately will raise his energy, increasing the chances that he'll run directly to you. When he reaches you, you can try backing up a few steps before rewarding him. By backing up a few steps, you're allowing him to chase you just a bit, which works as an additional primary reinforcement. In addition to this moment of play, you can reward him with treats and praise. At this point, you can hold onto your dog while your helper repeats the process. After a few minutes of this back and forth "game," your Papillon should understand the basics of the recall. You can then start increasing your distance and eventually working in environments with more distractions.

Off/Down

It's important to maintain your status as the leader of the pack, and to do so you may need to ask your Papillon to get out of your favorite chair. The 'off' or 'down' command is also useful if your dog attempts to develop bad habits such as jumping onto tables or guests' laps without their permission. Make sure you differentiate your commands for lying down and getting off furniture. If you use 'down' for lying down, you must use a different command such as 'off' to ask him to jump down.

There are a few ways to teach your dog to get off furniture. The first method is to use positive reinforcement only. As you give your command, lure your dog off the sofa or chair with a treat. Once all four paws are on the ground you can reward him with your primary and secondary reinforcements of choice. You can also combine positive reinforcement with negative reinforcement to further clarify your instructions to your dog. You can use a leash or slip lead and apply gentle pressure toward the edge of the couch. If you've worked with your dog on his leash skills before, he should understand your request. Once he jumps down, release the pressure and reward him. You can also scoot him toward the edge with your hand as you give the command and then reward him once he jumps off. If your dog has resource-guarding or aggression issues, you may need to avoid using your hand. Some dogs become defensive over their space and may bite, so use your best judgment when deciding which method to use.

Give/Drop

The 'give' or 'drop' command is important to your Papillon's basic household manners, but it's also important if he has a tendency to pick up items from the ground on your walk. If you plan on competing in obedience or dock diving, your dog will also need to have a solid understanding of this command. Dogs who are regularly asked to give up toys, chews, or items they've stolen are also less likely to develop resource-guarding issues.

If your dog has a high-value item in his mouth, it's not a good idea to just try to take it from him. He may not want to let go and may even snap at you when you try to take it. The best way to teach your dog that it's okay to give up items is to offer a trade. Decide what your command will be and give it as you offer your dog a treat. It may take a few repetitions

Photo Courtesy of Tom Barcik

before he understands that he's being rewarded for dropping the item. If your Papillon has resource-guarding issues, you may need to lure him away from the item with the treat in order to safely take it from him. If it's an item he's allowed to have, you can give it back to him immediately after rewarding him for dropping it. Once the item is back in his possession, you can try asking him to drop it again.

Walk

Good manners are not just important in the house. Your Papillon should be able to walk politely on the leash without pulling or resisting no matter where you take him. A dog that pulls on the leash is more likely to get excited when he sees strange dogs or people and he may develop bad habits such as excessive barking or aggression. If your dog wears a collar, he may seriously injure himself as well, so it's essential to teach him to walk politely next to you. There are many gimmicks on the market designed to discourage your dog from pulling, but the most effective method is patience and dedication to your training.

When walking your Papillon, do not reward him for any tension on the leash. If he begins pulling on the leash, simply stop walking. You can either wait for him to come back to you or call him back, but when he returns to a position where there is slack in the lead, give him a treat or praise him. After a few repetitions, your Papillon is likely to get impatient with so many stops. Eventually, he should understand that pulling on the leash results in an interruption in the walk, while keeping a loose leash allows the walk to continue. It may take several walks before your Papillon consistently keeps slack in the leash. If your dog is particularly excitable or energetic, it may be helpful to hold a quick play session before your walk to wear him out. A calmer dog will learn this skill much more quickly than one who is just excited to be outside. If your dog seems to struggle with polite leash manners, try practicing them around the house where there are fewer distractions.

Advanced Commands

As your Papillon progresses in his training, you can create more challenging versions of each of these basic commands. Stays can become longer, and polite walking can be done without a leash. If you're interested in competing in dog sports, you can work with a trainer on more advanced, sport-specific commands. If competition doesn't interest you, you can always teach your dog fun tricks. You can even do both by competing in the AKC's new trick dog classes. Papillons are incredibly intelligent dogs who are eager to learn, so the options for teaching them advanced commands are endless.

CHAPTER 12
Unwanted Behaviors

"Preventing unwanted behaviors is so much easier than trying to change an already established one. Put in the time the first year, keeping your puppy close. This will help prevent poor house training, chewing, nuisance barking, etc. and you will be rewarded for years to come."

Elyse Vandermolen
Clearlake Papillons

What is Bad Behavior in Dogs?

Bad behavior in dogs consists of unwanted, harmful, or destructive behaviors. Some bad habits are simply disruptive or disrespectful, such as excessive barking or poor leash manners. These behaviors are not likely to cause you or your Papillon any harm, but they are frustrating and can have a serious impact on your relationship with your dog. They may also escalate into more serious problems. Other bad habits can be incredibly dangerous for your Papillon. Habits such as bolting out an open door, eating trash, or aggression can lead to serious injury or even death. Aggressive behavior may also put you or your family members in danger of being bitten.

Bad habits usually develop out of seemingly harmless bad behavior that hasn't been corrected. Dogs don't start out with extreme behavior issues, it takes time and a lack of training for them to develop. It might be funny to see your tiny Papillon puppy growl at your neighbor, but if that behavior isn't corrected it can escalate into much more dangerous behavior that can be difficult to fix. When bad behavior is not consistently corrected, the dog doesn't understand that their actions are inappropriate. Even if the behavior is corrected on occasion, the dog is more likely to be confused rather than understand the correction. They wonder why they're allowed to display that behavior without correction sometimes, while at other times they're punished. Luckily, most bad behavior can be corrected with proper training, patience, and consistency.

*Photo Courtesy of
Merinda McCarty*

Finding the Root of the Problem

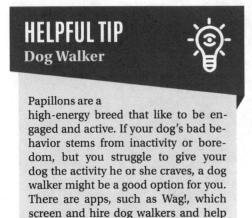

HELPFUL TIP
Dog Walker

Papillons are a high-energy breed that like to be engaged and active. If your dog's bad behavior stems from inactivity or boredom, but you struggle to give your dog the activity he or she craves, a dog walker might be a good option for you. There are apps, such as Wag!, which screen and hire dog walkers and help connect them with dog owners.

Finding the cause of your Papillon's unwanted behavior is essential to developing a plan to correct it. If you don't know why your dog is acting out, you'll never be able to completely fix the problem. If you know your dog's excessive barking begins when he sees people walking by outside, then you know where to focus your attention in his training. However, if you don't know why your dog is displaying aggressive behavior toward your guests, you won't be able to completely fix the problem. You may be able to temporarily fix the situation, but the behavior is likely to surface again in the future when the unknown stimuli causes your dog to react.

A potential cause for your Papillon's bad behavior may be your own behavior, so you may need to reflect on how your behavior affects your dog. Dogs, especially Papillons, are incredibly tuned in to their owners. If you are showing fear or stress in certain situations, it's possible your dog is picking up on your body language and he feels that there is a reason to react with fear or aggression. If you want your dog to show confidence in new situations, you must be confident as well. If you model the desired behavior, your dog is more likely to follow your lead. You must be willing to improve yourself in order to eliminate your dog's bad behavior.

Poor management of your dog's environment may also be the cause for your dog's bad habits. If you know your dog gets into trouble when he has access to the entire house while you're gone, then you need to limit his access to one room or even a playpen or crate. By controlling your dog's environment, you have better control over his behavior. Careful management is a lifetime commitment, so you must be willing to constantly examine your dog's environment to correct your dog's bad habits and prevent new ones from developing.

Bad Behavior Prevention

Photo Courtesy of Michael Sukovich

It's much easier to prevent bad behavior than it is to correct it. The key to preventing bad habits from developing in the first place is to manage your dog's environment and behavior. If you know your dog has a habit of getting into the trash when you leave the house, do not leave the trash in a place that he has access to. If your dog displays aggression toward the dog down the street, avoid that dog until your Papillon is further along in his training. Papillons are incredibly intelligent and it's important to stay one step ahead of them with your management. If you have any doubts about whether your dog can be trusted in a certain situation, err on the side of caution and make changes to his environment to prevent any problems.

It's crucial to be as consistent as possible in your dog's training to prevent him from developing bad habits. Allowing your dog to pull on the leash on some walks, while asking him to walk on a loose leash at other times will not teach him the proper behavior. Training your dog is a huge commitment and you must be prepared to work with your dog on a regular basis. You may not be motivated to train your dog every day, but your dog will certainly be motivated to develop bad habits in order to entertain himself. If you are consistent in your expectations and training, you can expect consistency in your dog's behavior. The only way to truly prevent bad habits from developing is to not allow your dog to perform those behaviors in the first place. If he knows he can't get away with bad behaviors, he'll lose interest in them quickly. Be aware that if you let him behave badly on occasion, he will never learn that it's a behavior that's not allowed; he'll just wonder why he gets punished for it every so often.

How to Properly Correct Your Dog

Photo Courtesy of
Leah Radley

When you correct your Papillon's bad behavior, it's important to do so correctly to avoid fearful or aggressive responses from your dog in the future. No matter how bad your dog's behavior is, it is never appropriate to hit or kick your dog. An aggressive response from you may be met with an aggressive response from your dog and he may bite you. You may inadvertently cause your dog to fear you, and possibly humans in general. Even the most extreme behavior can be improved with a gentle touch and positive reinforcement.

You must also remember that you cannot punish your dog if you don't catch him in the act. If you come home and find that your dog has chewed up your favorite shoes, you must simply clean up the mess and move on. However, if you catch your Papillon with your favorite shoes in his mouth, then it's appropriate to correct him. Be careful not to overcorrect your dog. Your correction must be enough to let him know that his behavior was wrong, but not so much that he becomes fearful.

Proper corrections include loud claps, stomps, or a firm 'no.' Some trainers also suggest filling a spray bottle with water and spritzing the dog in the face when he misbehaves. Most dogs hate water in their face so it's an effective correction but won't harm the dog. This is a stronger correction than a simple 'no,' so use your best judgment on whether it's necessary for your dog's specific behavior. The only situation in which you may need a harsher correction would be to interrupt a dog fight. In this case, you may need to yell loudly, spray them with water, or use a loud noise such as a whistle or air horn. Papillons can be seriously injured or even killed in a fight, so it's appropriate to use a stronger correction in this situation.

Fixing Bad Habits

The most important aspects of correcting bad habits are patience and dedication. Bad habits do not develop overnight, and they will not be corrected overnight. It may take weeks, or even months, of consistent training to completely correct your Papillon's bad behavior. Whether you are tackling the challenge on your own or working with a professional trainer, you need to understand that it will take time for your dog to develop new behaviors. Depending on the specific problem behavior, it may take a few days or weeks before you even notice much improvement. It can be easy to lose motivation and get frustrated with your dog when you don't see huge improvements at first, but you must be patient.

You must be also dedicated to your Papillon's training, no matter how much work it is. You may come home after a long day of work and feel like taking the day off from your dog's training, but if you truly want to fix your Papillon's bad habits, you must be consistent. Allowing your dog to get away with bad habits even infrequently can result in major setbacks in your training. Inconsistency in training is what allowed the bad habits to develop in the first place, so you must be dedicated and consistent in your corrections. Even after your dog's behavior has improved, you must continually manage your dog's environment and behavior to prevent any lapses in bad habits. Certain bad habits may require a lifetime of management, so be prepared to dedicate a lot of time and work to fixing your dog's bad behavior.

Photo Courtesy of
Sue Dempster

When to Call a Professional

Do not be afraid to call a professional whenever you think you could use a helping hand. Even if it's a relatively simple problem, it can easily escalate into a more difficult or even dangerous situation if you don't deal with it. Even if a behavior isn't particularly dangerous, it can be frustrating to live with a difficult dog. Bad manners can cause a rift in your relationship with your dog and with your family members. Even if you're struggling with simple bad behaviors such as bolting out an open door or pulling on the leash, a trainer will be able to evaluate the situation and give you a training plan to follow. Professional trainers deal with a variety of problem behaviors on a daily basis and they will be happy to work with you to figure out a solution, but it's important to seek help at the first sign of bad behavior.

If your dog is consistently displaying aggressive, destructive, or fearful behavior, you need to seek professional advice as soon as possible. These types of behavior can be difficult to manage and can escalate quickly, possibly with dangerous or deadly consequences. Fearful and aggressive behavior in particular can be incredibly difficult for the average dog owner to correct. Papillons often forget how small they are and may display aggression toward bigger dogs. If they display aggression toward humans, even a small dog can cause serious injury, especially if it bites a child. Fearful behavior can also progress into aggression if the dog feels the need to defend himself. Professional trainers can work with you and your dog to determine the source of his behavior and develop a plan to correct it.

Papillon-Specific Bad Habits

Papillons are well-known for their stubborn attitudes. One of their most common bad behaviors is their resistance to house-training. Like many other small breeds, they're not impossible to house-train, but it will take a significant amount of time and training to completely train them. Even Papillons who are usually trustworthy indoors may experience a lapse in their training in inclement weather. Papillons enjoy being clean, and they will often opt to relieve themselves indoors rather than get their feet wet outside.

It's common for Papillons to find their way into trouble, especially if they don't receive the proper amount of physical and mental exercise. They may steal laundry, such as socks and underwear, and spread it throughout the house or chew it up. Papillons are also notorious for getting into the trash. Managing these bad behaviors is as simple as keeping things out of your dog's reach. Put your laundry in a hamper and your trash can inside a cabinet, or purchase one that's tall enough and heavy enough that your Papillon can't knock it over.

Papillons' self-confidence can be both a positive and negative trait. On the negative side, they may develop dominant behaviors and may try to bully other dogs. They may growl at, hump, or nip at other dogs. With more submissive dogs, they may get away with it, but with another dominant dog it can result in a fight, especially if the other dog is bigger. Proper management of your dog's behavior is key to preventing your Papillon from becoming a bully and getting himself into a dangerous situation.

CHAPTER 13
Traveling with Papillons

"They make wonderful travel companions as they are small enough to take anywhere. They will learn to know when it is time to go and will get very excited. Papillons just want to be with their owners, they are like your shadow."

Sally Howard
Tiny T Papillons / K's Klassic Ponies

Dog Carriers and Car Restraints

There are several different ways to keep your Papillon restrained inside of your vehicle. Certain types of carriers or barriers work better in different cars, so you may need to find one to fit your specific vehicle. You may also need to try out a few different options to see which you and your Papillon prefer. Some dogs prefer the security of a covered carrier or crate, while others prefer to be in a booster seat, so they can look out the window. As your Papillon becomes more comfortable, you may be able to adjust your carrier preferences if needed.

If you prefer that your dog remain in an enclosed space for the duration of the car trip, consider the different varieties of carriers available on the market. There are soft-sided or hard-sided varieties available in a range of prices, so consider your budget before deciding which type of carrier you'd prefer. For soft-sided carriers, there are smaller, portable carriers that can be seat-belted in for security. There are also square crate-type carriers, or long, tube-shaped carriers that run the entire length of the backseat. A regular wire or plastic crate also makes a great car carrier. A few companies also make heavy-duty metal crates that are intended to withstand the impact of a car crash, but they can be quite expensive. No matter which type of carrier you choose, be sure that it's large enough for your dog to comfortably stand up and turn around. If you have multiple dogs and plan to travel with them in the same carrier, make sure it's big enough for them to each have a comfortable amount of room. It's also important that your dog is properly crate trained before adding the stress of travel. If your dog isn't comfortable in a crate, he or she may react badly once the car starts moving, so do your homework and properly prepare your dog for traveling in a crate.

Photo Courtesy of Archa Emerson

If you would prefer that your Papillon have more freedom than a carrier allows, it's still important to keep him safe while you're driving. Many owners opt to keep their dogs in the backseat or the cargo area of their vehicle by using a barrier. These barriers are usually made of a metal mesh or bar, but there are fabric varieties available as well. Depending on the type of car you drive and your dog's behavior in the car, you can decide what works best for you and your Papillon. The downside of barriers is that you need to be cautious when opening and closing the car doors once you've arrived at your destination. Without an actual restraint, your dog can easily jump out and run off if you aren't careful.

Seat belts are another great option for safe traveling by car. Doggie seatbelts consist of a short leash with a seatbelt latchplate on one end that simply clips into your car's seat-belt buckle. The other end of the leash attaches to your dog's harness. It's advisable to use a harness with a seat belt, rather than a collar, because in the case of an accident or hard braking, your dog can be seriously injured if his collar is the only thing attached to the car. Since Papillons are quite small, there are also booster seats available to give them a lift. These booster seats usually attach to the car seat with the seat belt, but they also have an additional seat-belt buckle or attached leash that you can snap to your dog's harness.

No matter which method of restraint you use, it's important to keep your dog contained while in the car. Riding in your lap, or loose in the car, can be dangerous for both you and the dog. Small dogs, such as Papillons, can easily fall on the floor beneath your feet while you're driving. In the case of an accident, an unrestrained dog may be seriously injured in the impact. They may also be able to escape the damaged vehicle and run off or be further injured in traffic. Papillons are excellent travel companions, but just like your human family members, they must follow the rules for car safety.

Preparing Your Dog for Car Rides

Photo Courtesy of Kade Peterson

Before you take your Papillon on a road trip, consider his or her previous experiences with traveling by car. If your dog is an experienced traveler, he may be able to eat and drink on the road with no problem. If he is new to traveling, however, you may want to limit his food and water consumption before you get on the road. Some dogs can experience car sickness, especially if they've had a big meal or bowl of water. As a precaution, consider bringing along extra towels or blankets in case your dog does get sick. You can also consider purchasing a waterproof seat cover if your dog is traveling with a seat belt or behind a barrier. Carriers are usually much easier to clean, so if your Papillon frequently becomes sick while traveling, it may be easier to travel with him inside of his crate.

Be sure to give your dog a potty break before beginning your trip and every few hours while on the road. Just like at home, you'll need to stick to the usual schedule to prevent accidents. With puppies, this can mean stopping every couple hours. If you are just traveling across town, or the drive isn't long, your adult Papillon should be able to make the entire trip without stopping.

As with other aspects of safe road travel, double-check all carriers, barriers, or seat belts before leaving. Make sure everything is functioning as it should and that you have all your dog's necessary supplies. If you're traveling for several days or longer, be sure that you have any collars, leashes, bowls, and waste bags, as well as enough food and water. Being prepared will help ensure that both you and your Papillon enjoy traveling together.

Flying and Hotel Stays

When booking air travel or hotel stays, make sure that the airline or hotel allows dogs. If they don't, you have time to make the necessary arrangements. Finding this information out at the last minute can be disastrous. Both airlines and hotels may also charge extra fees for the dog, so be sure to budget for this when you're making travel plans.

Papillons are small dogs, so they are often able to travel in the cabin of the plane, rather than in the cargo area. Most airlines require a certain size and type of bag, but these rules can vary depending on the airline or type of plane, so be sure to ask your airline representative or travel agent. Hard plastic or soft-sided carriers are usually recommended. Make sure your Papillon has enough room to comfortably stand up and turn around. If your carrier is too small or too big, you may not be allowed to travel.

HELPFUL TIP
Nervous Bladder

Flying can be stressful for anyone, especially your dog. Even the most seasoned travelers sometimes deal with anxiety when boarding a plane. In the case of a nervous bladder, you may want to line your dog's crate or carrier with a moisture-wicking liner, such as DryFur, to keep your pet comfortable even after a nervous bladder mishap.

Most airlines also request that the dog stay in the carrier under the seat in front of you for the duration of the flight, so make sure your dog is comfortable with traveling in the carrier. In the weeks or months before travel, get him comfortable with lying quietly in the carrier. You can take him for short walks around the house or neighborhood, or even to the local pet store or café. The more time he spends in the carrier, the more comfortable he will be once you've boarded the plane.

Many hotels across the country are considered to be dog-friendly. Some even provide beds and water dishes for their canine guests, while others are just happy to have you stay with them. No matter their level of dog friendliness, it's important for your dog to be a respectful guest. If you bring a barking, wild dog who isn't house-trained into a hotel, you may not be allowed to stay, or you may encounter additional fees. If you've done your homework with training and socializing at home, however, you and your Papillon should be welcomed guests at any pet-friendly establishment.

Photo Courtesy of Matt Glaser

Kenneling vs. Dog Sitters

Travel can be stressful, especially when you can't bring your Papillon with you. Finding the perfect boarding kennel or dog sitter can help relieve that stress for both you and your dog. When searching for the ideal place to take care of your Papillon in your absence, don't just settle on the first place you visit. Interview the boarding kennel staff or dog sitter to make sure it's the right fit for your precious pooch. Some boarding kennels offer playgroups or individual walks or playtime, so consider whether your dog would prefer to play with a group of dogs or with an individual staff member. Depending on your area, you may even find kennels that are cage-free, where the facility is staffed 24/7 and the dogs are not kept in kennels. If you think your dog would prefer a homier environment, consider hiring a dog sitter. Most dog sitters will either watch your dog in their own home or stay at your house while you're away. Based on your Papillon's individual personality, decide what environment is going to be more comfortable for him until you return home.

Depending on your budget and the area in which you live, you will likely find a variety of boarding options available. Basic boarding kennels will be the cheapest options. These facilities keep your dog in a simple cage or run and provide him with two or three potty breaks per day. If you have multiple dogs, they will often allow all your dogs to stay in the same kennel. Most of these facilities are not staffed overnight. Higher-end boarding facilities will offer more options but will likely be more expensive. Some kennels provide elevated beds, televisions, and playgroups or individual attention. If your Papillon is quite social, playgroups can be an excellent way to keep your dog busy and well exercised while you're away. A new trend in boarding facilities is cage-free boarding. The facility is staffed around the clock and dogs can play, sleep, and eat with their new friends.

If a kennel environment seems too stressful for your Papillon, consider hiring a dog sitter. Many companies exist that hire individual sitters to stay with the dogs, usually in your home. Self-employed pet sitters may also be willing to keep your dog in their own home, if you'd prefer. If you have other pets, or plants that need watered, a pet sitter can help keep your household running smoothly in your absence. Many sitters are happy to bring in your mail, water your lawn, and maintain the security of your home. Not having to leave home can also ease the stress with more sensitive pets. Pet sitters can be more expensive than many boarding kennels, but generally vary based on the services they provide.

Whether you choose a boarding kennel or pet sitter, it's important to thoroughly interview the staff and tour the facility or pet sitter's home

Photo Courtesy of
Merinda McCarty

before you leave your Papillon. Make sure the place is well-staffed and sanitary. Ask them if you can bring your dog's food, bedding, and toys to make him feel more at home. If you do bring items from home, be sure to write your name or your dog's name on everything or make a list to make sure that you get everything back at the end of the stay. Inquire about the daily feeding and potty break schedule. A good sitter or boarding kennel should be willing to take your dog out for potty breaks at least three times per day. If your dog will be allowed to play with other dogs, make sure there are enough staff members for the size of the playgroup. You may also want to ask if they separate the dogs by size, age, or energy level. It can be dangerous for a tiny Papillon to be in a group with overly enthusiastic large dogs. You may also want to consider a trial day before you leave. Ask the boarding kennel or pet sitter if they can take care of your dog for a day. That way, if any problems arise, you can pick your dog up immediately. If everything goes well, you can feel comfortable leaving your Papillon in the hands of a caring and capable sitter or boarding kennel.

Tips and Tricks for Traveling

Papillons love spending time with their family, and travel is no exception. If it's possible to take your dog with you, your Papillon will be happy to accompany you anywhere you go. However, it's important to thoroughly prepare your family and your dog for any travel together. Karen Lawrence of MCK Papillons says, "Papillons are small and travel very well if started when young." As soon as possible, begin acclimating your dog to the car or kennel. The more time you spend preparing, the easier it will be to travel when the time comes. Proper socialization will also make traveling much easier. The more experiences you can expose your Papillon to, the better prepared he'll be when you encounter new faces and places on your adventures together.

CHAPTER 14
Nutrition

"All dogs fed a species appropriate diet enjoy better health and teeth. I prefer a raw diet for all of my Papillons plus some supplementation - nutritional yeast, lecithin, kelp, alfalfa, vitamin C."

Elyse Vandermolen
Clearlake Papillons

Importance of a Good Diet

A properly balanced diet is essential to your Papillon's overall health and well-being. Without a proper diet, your dog is at risk for developing serious and often life-threatening conditions, especially as a growing puppy. The vitamins and minerals in a good diet allow a dog's body to build and maintain strong bones and muscles, a healthy brain, and a soft and shiny coat. Fats and protein help keep the dogs' bodies in shape and give them the energy to perform in the show ring or to keep you company on walks around the neighborhood. Good nutrition also helps boost your dog's immune system, keeping him safe from disease.

Obesity is by far the most common diet-related health problem facing modern dogs. A properly balanced diet is important, but so is portion control and adequate exercise. If a dog does not receive a balanced diet, he can develop serious conditions such as pancreatitis, bladder or kidney stones, or even heart disease. Some dogs may also develop food intolerances or allergies over time.

Many pet food companies label their food as being appropriate for dogs in all life stages. Depending on your dog, this may or may not be appropriate. As a dog ages or develops certain health problems, it's important to change his diet accordingly, so don't expect to feed your dog the same food for his entire life. Some companies offer puppy food for growing young dogs, which typically contain more calories and a different ratio of certain nutrients. Puppy food is typically fed until a dog is be-

Photo Courtesy of
Alexandra Perry

tween nine and twelve months of age. Senior dog food is also available for dogs that require fewer calories and more fiber and joint support.

Commercial pet foods are scientifically developed to provide the necessary nutrients for healthy growth and development. They are required by law to meet a certain standard of pet nutrition and can be recalled if the food is found to be substandard. Many Papillon owners have also found success in homemade cooked or raw diets, often working with qualified pet nutritionists to develop a properly balanced diet at home. Homemade meals are often quite labor intensive, so consider whether you're willing to dedicate a large portion of your free time to making dog food. No matter which type of food you choose, make sure it's properly balanced to ensure your Papillon is receiving all of the necessary nutrients for a healthy life.

Good Foods for Papillons

The dog food and treat section can be overwhelming when trying to decide what's best for your Papillon. Unfortunately, there is no perfect food. What works well for one dog may not work for another. The key is to understand your Papillon as an individual and choose a food that suits him best. You may need to try a few different products before you find one that works. If your dog has any food sensitivities or health problems, take this into consideration when choosing food and treats. Some types of food can make certain health problems worse, so if you have any doubts, ask your veterinarian.

When deciding what to feed your Papillon, consider your budget in terms of both time and money. If you have a full-time job and hobbies, it may be difficult for you to find time to prepare a homemade meal for your dog. Commercial food may be easier to feed, but it is available in a wide variety of price points. Novel protein and grain-free kibbles tend to be expensive, but the ingredients in low-priced kibble may not agree with all dogs. Commercial refrigerated or raw food can also be quite expensive. Luckily, Papillons are small and eat considerably less than their large-breed cousins.

If you do need to change your Papillon's food, remember to do so slowly. Mix in 25 percent of the new food with 75 percent of the old food for a few feedings. Then you can feed 50 percent new food with 50 percent old food for the next few meals. Finally, you may feed 75 percent new food with 25 percent old food for the final meals of the transition. After about five to seven days, you can feed your dog 100 percent new food. Switching too fast can cause digestive upset and may cause your Papillon to have accidents in the house. A slow transition will help prevent stomach problems in most dogs.

Different Types of Commercial Food

When you think of commercial dog food, you likely think of kibble first. The small, crunchy nuggets are by far the most popular type of commercial food. There are a nearly endless variety of options depending on your dog's individual needs. There are different types of kibble for the different life stages and some companies even have different formulas based on breed. Grain-free kibble is trending, with carbohydrates such as potatoes and peas replacing traditional grains such as wheat and corn.

FUN FACT
Let Them Eat Cake

It often feels as if the dog is a member of the family, so it's only fitting that you give your dog an extra treat on his or her birthday. Dog bakeries are springing up all over the place, and many offer decadent treats for your furry companions' special occasions. Dog bakeries are required to adhere to federal standards for pet food, but never hesitate to ask what goes into their treats to make sure your dog is getting the best ingredients.

As more dogs develop food intolerances and allergies, kibble manufacturers are answering the call with novel proteins such as salmon and kangaroo. You can find tiny kibble for toy breeds and large kibble intended to help clean teeth. If your dog has kidney, joint, or heart problems you can even find specific diets to help his condition, but these are often only available from your veterinarian. There are even low-calorie kibbles available for dogs who need to trim their waist line. No matter your dog's needs, there's a specific formula of kibble available. In addition to the wide variety, another benefit of kibble is that the crunchy pieces tend to help scrape plaque and tartar off your dog's teeth. This can be particularly beneficial to small breeds who are prone to dental problems. Unfortunately, some dogs can be a little fussy with kibble, so if you have a picky Papillon you may need to try a few before finding one that your dog enjoys.

Canned food is softer than kibble but is available in nearly as many varieties. Dogs often find canned food to be more palatable so it's a great option for fussy dogs or older dogs who may struggle with crunchy food. It also contains more moisture, so it can help with dogs who tend to drink less water than they should. Some canned food is also more calorie dense, so you may need to adjust your portion size accordingly. As with kibble, there are different types for different needs, including condition-specific varieties available only from your veterinarian. The downside of canned food is that it tends to adhere to the dog's teeth, so you need to be more diligent about brushing your dog's teeth or providing

Photo Courtesy of
Matt Glaser

dental toys or chews. Dogs who strictly eat canned food may need to see a veterinarian for a professional dental cleaning more often as well.

A new trend in dog food can be found in the refrigerated section of your local pet store. Fresh-cooked dog food is a great choice for owners who want to feed their dogs a homemade diet, but simply don't have the time or the means to do so. This type of food is generally softer than kibble, though often not as soft as canned food. It's packaged into rolls which can be sliced into appropriately sized portions as needed and placed back in the refrigerator until the next meal. This type of food can also be more expensive than traditional kibble and canned food diets, so take your budget into consideration when choosing your dog's diet.

Your local pet store may also have a freezer section containing commercial raw dog food. Raw dog food is rising in popularity with pet owners who believe they should feed their pets the same diet as their ancestors ate. Commercial raw diets are typically a nutritionally balanced mixture of meat, organs, bones, and vegetables. These diets do not generally contain any grains or excess carbohydrates. They are usually available in either small nuggets or patties. Along with the raw food in the freezer section, you may find raw bones for recreational chewing and goat's milk to supplement the raw diet. Many raw feeders provide their dogs with recreational chews to make up for the soft nuggets or patties that can cause tartar buildup. Commercial raw diets are also available in a variety of proteins to give options for dogs with food sensitivities.

Homemade Foods and Recipes

Many Papillon owners choose to make their own dog food. Some owners choose to prepare raw diets for their Papillons, while others prefer to cook. Homemade diets can be more expensive and more labor intensive, so it's important to consider how much time, effort, and money you're willing to spend on your dog's diet. Proper balance in homemade diets is essential to your dog's health. Diet imbalances typically do not show up immediately and you may see long-term effects on your Papillon's health. If you are unsure about whether your homemade diet is nutritionally balanced, consider consulting a professional pet nutritionist or your veterinarian. They will be able to give you accurate information on your dog's diet and can tell you whether you need to make any changes.

Raw diets are the most popular type of homemade food. They are typically divided into two categories: Biologically Appropriate Raw Food, or BARF, and Prey Model Raw, or PMR. BARF diets and PMR diets differ in that BARF diets allow for a certain percentage of vegetables, while PMR diets do not. PMR diets are intended to reflect the meat, bone, and organ content of whole prey animals. Some owners also choose to supplement their dog's diet with goat's milk, bone broth, or fish stock to provide variety and additional nutrients. It's important to consider your dog's size when feeding a homemade raw diet. Dogs on this diet will be consuming bone, which can be difficult for petite dogs, so many toy breed owners choose to grind their dog's food. As with commercial raw diets, recreational bones, chews, or toys must be provided for teeth cleaning purposes.

Cooked diets are also a great choice for Papillons, particularly for more picky dogs. Some dogs will refuse to eat kibble, canned, or raw diets, but will gobble up home cooked meals. Homemade cooked diets are similar to raw diets and typically contain meat, organs, and vegetables. Some owners also choose to add carbohydrates such as rice, oatmeal, or barley. Most balanced meals will contain a certain percentage of protein, fat, and carbohydrates, but they may require additional supplements such as eggshells, kelp powder, or dairy products. There are many books available on the market that can provide well-researched, balanced recipes to try out with your dog. One of the benefits of cooking your own dog food is that you can tailor the recipes to your dog's individual needs and preferences.

People Food – Harmful and Acceptable Kinds

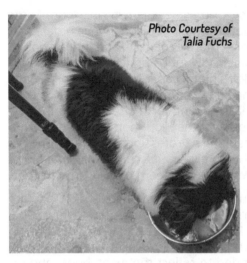

Photo Courtesy of Talia Fuchs

Fruits and vegetables can be beneficial to Papillons, no matter what their main diet is. They make great snacks and training rewards. Most dogs love vegetables like carrots, peas, broccoli, and even sweet potatoes. Many dogs also enjoy green beans, spinach, and cucumbers. Fruit can also be a tasty treat, but it's often higher in sugar, so it must be fed in moderation. Dog-safe fruits include blueberries, strawberries, watermelon, apples, and bananas. Pineapple, cantaloupe, and raspberries are also healthy for dogs. Not all fruits and vegetables are safe for dogs though. Grapes, onions, garlic, and avocado can be harmful if ingested. Beware of any pitted fruit, as the pits are often toxic to dogs as well as being a choking hazard. If the pit is removed, fruits like mangoes, cherries, and peaches can be fed without concern.

Some people food is acceptable for dogs to eat, but only in small amounts. Peanut butter and cheese are popular treats, but they must be fed in moderation. They are high in fat and can have a negative impact on your dog's endocrine system. Foods that are heavy in salt, such as ham and popcorn, should also be fed sparingly. Some dogs do well with dairy, while other may display symptoms of lactose intolerance, so depending on your dog, you may also want to limit foods like milk, yogurt, and kefir.

Everyone knows that chocolate is toxic for dogs, but there are other people foods that be dangerous, or even deadly, if consumed. Coffee, or any food containing caffeine, can be fatal if your dog eats enough of it. Pets are more sensitive to caffeine than humans are, so even a relatively small amount can be dangerous. Foods that contain the sugar replacement xylitol are also toxic to dogs. Sugar-free candies and gum often contain this deadly ingredient. Alcohol can also be deadly, so be sure to keep your dog away from the liquor cabinet. If your dog does consume any harmful people food, call your local poison control or emergency veterinary clinic right away. The sooner your pet can be treated, the more likely he is to survive.

Weight Management

The most common health concern among pets is obesity. Obesity can cause a multitude of other conditions and can severely limit your dog's ability to exercise and enjoy life. It's also hard on weight-bearing joints and can lead to arthritis even in younger dogs. The best way to prevent weight problems is to closely monitor your Papillon's weight and portion sizes. It may be tempting to feed your pooch every time he begs for it, but for the sake of your dog's health, you must resist. When looking down at your dog from above, see if your dog has a defined waistline. This can be difficult to see in Papillons as they have so much hair, so you may need to put your hands on the dog to see if you can feel a well-defined waist. The ribs should also be easily felt, but not seen. From the side, a dog's belly should tuck up at the waist when at an appropriate weight. If you have any questions about whether your dog is at an appropriate weight, talk to your veterinarian.

When you are determining your Papillon's portion sizes for the day, don't forget about the treats. It's easy to forget that extra serving of treats during your dog's daily training session, but it can have a major effect on his waistline if it's not counted in his calorie allotment. If you're worried about the number of calories your dog is receiving during your training sessions, try substituting his treats for a small amount of kibble. By taking a portion of his breakfast or dinner and using it for training, you're keeping his calories in check while still giving him a tasty reward for good behavior. You may also substitute his training treats with healthier options such as chopped fruit or vegetables. Just be sure to limit the amount of fruit you feed, as it can be high in sugar.

Portion sizes are a key factor in achieving the ideal weight, but proper exercise is equally important. The more exercise your dog gets, the more calories he burns. This means he can eat more, so if you're worried about restricting his calories too much, just take your Papillon for longer walks or play sessions. A well-exercised dog is a happy dog, so don't be afraid to go that extra mile.

CHAPTER 15
Grooming Your Papillon

Coat Basics

Papillons are a single-coated breed, which means that they do not have the heavy undercoat common to breeds such as Huskies and Golden Retrievers. Their long, silky coat has the appearance of being difficult to care for, but Papillons are rather low maintenance in terms of their grooming needs. The breed rarely has that "doggie" odor found in other types of dog.

Amanda Vidrine of Earth Angels Papillons describes the breed as moderate shedders. She says, "It is worse in the spring when the dogs are getting rid of the thick winter coat. Brushing at this time helps a great deal. It does get bad again in the late summer/early fall to prepare for the winter, but it is not as bad as in the spring." She also advises, "Females that are not spayed may have shedding after a heat cycle, so I recommend spaying a female that is bought as a pet. Her coat will come in nicely and be more stable."

Bathing and Brushing

"Make sure to have their toe nails and hair trimmed at least once a month. A Papillon with a proper coat does not matt easily, so a weekly brushing and a monthly bath with keep them looking great."

Karen Lawrence
MCK Papillons

Papillons are relatively easy to care for in that they require very little as far as grooming. Although more frequent brushing may be needed at certain times during the year, most Papillon owners find success with weekly brushing. Be sure to focus on the dog's ear fringe, the insides of the hind legs, and the long hair on the back of the thighs, commonly known as "culottes." These areas tend to have softer, finer hair that mats more easily. During times of heavier shedding, you may find that brushing every day or even every other day will help to minimize the hair found throughout your house. Some Papillons have a tendency to mat more quickly during seasonal shedding, so more frequent brushing can also help prevent mats from developing out of the dead hair.

Photo Courtesy of
Danielle Rexroad

When brushing your Papillon, the right tool will make the job easier and you and your Papillon will come to enjoy this time together. A slicker brush can be a great addition to your toolbox. These wire brushes work well with the breed's silky soft coat. Use caution when using the slicker brush, however, as too much pressure can scratch your dog's skin. Try to get through the whole coat, down to the skin, without scratching or scraping your Papillon's delicate skin. Metal combs are excellent for double-checking your work. You can comb down to the skin without having to worry as much about scratching. Brushing down to the skin is essential to removing all tangles from the coat and preventing mats from developing. If you notice a tangle or mat and your dog resists brushing, try holding the coat close to the skin with one hand while brushing

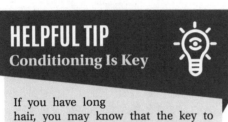

HELPFUL TIP

Conditioning Is Key

If you have long hair, you may know that the key to keeping your hair silky and smooth is using a quality conditioner. Though Papillons are not known for matting, conditioning their fur will help to maintain a luxurious and healthy coat. Just make sure to thoroughly rinse conditioner out of your dog's fur when bathing. Conditioning spray can also be used during brushing to tease out tangled hair.

with the other. This way you aren't pulling on your Papillon's hair. If a mat is too big and difficult to brush out, it's okay to cut it out. It's better to remove this small amount of hair before it causes larger problems. Use round-tipped scissors and extreme caution when cutting out a mat. If in doubt, your local groomer would be happy to help you with mat removal.

Papillons are relatively low-odor dogs and do not require frequent bathing. Most breeders recommend bathing every three to four weeks. Bathing too frequently can dry out the skin and coat, causing dandruff and itching. Infrequent bathing can also cause skin problems due to the buildup of dirt and natural oils on the skin.

There are many types of shampoo available depending on your dog's needs and your own preferences. Many companies make gentler puppy shampoos, while others focus on specific needs such as itchiness, odor control, or shedding. Look for a shampoo with more natural ingredients. The fewer chemicals in the product, the less likely it will be to cause skin irritation. Shampoos with more natural ingredients sometimes do not produce as many bubbles as shampoos with more artificial ingredients, but don't worry, they are still getting the dog clean. If your Papillon gets his feet dirty or is not dirty enough to require a full bath, consider purchasing a waterless shampoo to keep him clean between baths. These products are usually sprayed on

Photo Courtesy of Matt Glaser

and wiped off along with the dirt and grime. They leave your dog smelling fresh without the hassle of a full bath.

Photo Courtesy of
Elsa Rún Árnadóttir

Some owners choose to follow the shampoo with the conditioner of their choice, but it's not always necessary. If your dog is shedding heavily or matting frequently, an appropriate conditioner can help. If your dog has a soft, shiny, and healthy coat, a conditioner is not necessary. Leave-in spray conditioners are also great for detangling and conditioning the coat.

When you bathe your Papillon it's important to wash down to the skin. If you wash only the top hair, the coat's natural oils and dirt from the environment can cause irritation and mats. It can be difficult with long-haired breeds to get the shampoo down to the skin, so try parting the hair and shampooing in sections to ensure that each part of the dog is thoroughly cleaned. You also need to make sure that you don't get any shampoo in the dog's eyes or ears. If you're worried about getting soap in your dog's eyes, have some eye rinse on hand to quickly rinse out your dog's eyes if necessary. Some groomers place cotton balls in the dog's ears to prevent excess water from running into the ear canals. Just remember to remove the cotton balls when you're done bathing. Rinsing is also essential in preventing skin irritation, so be sure to rinse your dog's coat thoroughly. Professional groomers recommend rinsing your dog until you think the soap is gone, and then rinsing again. Make sure there are no traces of soap in your dog's coat. Many Papillons enjoy being dried with a warm hair dryer, while others prefer a simply towel dry and a running lap through the house. If you do choose to dry your dog with a hair dryer, hold it far enough away from the dog that you do not burn him, or simply use the cool air setting if your dryer has one.

Trimming the Nails

There are two methods of trimming the nails, and both have their pros and cons. Using a traditional scissor-type nail clipper is the more popular method. Most Papillon owners find them easy to use and effective. Groomers do not generally recommend guillotine-style nail trimmers as they can crush the nail rather than cut it, which can lead to pain and resistance from the dog. The downside to traditional nail clippers is that it can be very easy to cut the nail too short. Cutting the dog's "quick," or the nail's blood supply can be painful for the dog and messy. The other method to nail trimming is to use a grinder. Grinders allow you to take just a layer off at a time, reducing the risk of going too short. You are also able to round the edges of the nail, which can prevent your dog from scratching you, your family, and your furniture. They do require caution, as it is easy to get a Papillon's long coat stuck in the spinning head of the grinder. Most grinders have an automatic shutoff when this happens, but it can still be painful for the dog and take out a good chunk of coat. Many dogs prefer one method over the other, so you may want to try both to see what you prefer.

How often you trim your Papillon's nails will depend on a few different factors. Many breeders and owners recommend trimming a dog's nails every week, while others go two to three weeks between trims. Some owners even choose to trim nails monthly, along with the dog's monthly bath. If you walk your dog on pavement a lot, you may not need to trim the nails very often, as the pavement will help wear the nails down. Some dogs' nails also grow faster than others, so pay attention to how quickly your Papillon's nails seem to grow and trim accordingly.

To trim your Papillon's nails correctly, take a look at his nails and note where you see the "quick" or blood supply, and how far it descends into the nail. You want to avoid clipping this if possible. Having your dog on an elevated surface, such as a grooming table or countertop, can make the process easier, but be sure to keep a hand on your dog at all times to prevent him from jumping off. Regardless of whether you're using clippers or a grinder, lift up your dog's paw and brush back the paw hair to see the nail. See how far down the quick is and take just a small layer of the tip of the nail off at a time. If your dog stands politely, praise him and give him a reward if you'd like. By taking small layers off, you're less likely to cut the quick than if you take larger pieces of the nail. Once you begin to notice a darker circle in the center of the end of the nail, you've nearly reached the quick and it's time to move on to the next nail.

If you have any questions about nail trimming, ask your groomer or veterinarian for advice. If you'd rather not risk hurting your dog, or simply would rather not deal with it, take your Papillon to your local veterinary clinic or grooming shop. Nail trims are inexpensive, and most places offer the option of either a traditional clipper or grinder. The professionals are also more adept at handling difficult dogs, so if you are struggling to trim your dog's nails, it may be best to consult a groomer or vet. If you are struggling with your dog's behavior while trimming nails, it's best to seek help sooner rather than later. The sooner your vet or groomer can begin teaching your dog how to stand patiently, the less work it will be for them, and the less stress it will be for your dog.

Brushing Their Teeth

Teeth brushing must be done on a daily basis to have any real effect on a dog's dental health. With practice, this process can be quick and easy to do as part of your daily schedule. Daily brushing will help prevent plaque and tartar buildup on your Papillon's teeth. Excess tartar can result in serious health conditions, so it's important to take the necessary steps to keep your dog's mouth as healthy as possible. The bacteria present in tartar can lead to inflammation of the gums, or gingivitis, and eventually to periodontal disease. Dogs with periodontal disease can experience pain, inability to eat, and even tooth loss if not treated. The bacteria can also enter the bloodstream and infect vital organs such as the heart, liver, and kidneys. However, with regular dental care at home and by your veterinarian, periodontal disease is easily preventable.

Your local pet store or favorite online retailer likely has a few different options for canine toothbrushes and toothpastes. Toothbrushes similar in shape to the ones you use work well, or there are small rubber brushes that fit nicely on the end of your finger. Just make sure to find one that is appropriate for a Papillon's petite mouth. Toothpastes are usually available in a variety of flavors, but you must never use a toothpaste intended for human use. The ingredients in human toothpaste can be harmful to a dog, so if you don't have any toothpaste on hand you may make a paste out of baking soda and water. You may also find certain types of toys and treats intended to help scrape plaque and tartar off your dog's teeth. If your dog enjoys chewing on toys or treats, this can be a helpful addition to your dental care routine.

Even with daily brushing at home, your dog may still need to have a professional dental cleaning once in a while. Without daily at-home care, most veterinarians recommend a cleaning every 6-12 months. Your Papillon will undergo anesthesia for this procedure, but your vet will do a thorough health exam before the dental cleaning to ensure that your dog is healthy enough to proceed. It can be a worrisome time for caring owners, but with modern advances in veterinary medicine, anesthesia is incredibly safe and there is a low risk for problems in healthy animals.

Cleaning Ears and Eyes

Papillons are not particularly prone to ear infections, but the drop ears of the Phalène may cause more frequent ear problems. This is due to the ear leather covering the ear canal and restricting airflow. If a small amount of moisture enters the ear, such as during a bath or a swim, it can create the perfect environment for yeast and bacteria. To prevent infection, it's best to clean your dog's ears regularly. This should be done after every bath or swim. If you notice your dog itching his ears, or there is any redness or swelling, your dog may already have an infection. A simple trip to the vet for an examination and the appropriate medication will solve the problem.

There are many types of ear cleaner on the market, so your choice will mainly be based on personal preference. Your vet or groomer will be happy to recommend a specific cleaner for your dog's individual needs if you're having trouble choosing. Regardless of the brand, choose one that does not contain any alcohol. Alcohol can cause a burning sensation, especially with irritated or inflamed ears. Your dog will be much more cooperative if you don't cause him any pain.

When cleaning your Papillon's ears, wet a cotton ball in your chosen ear cleaner. Squeeze out any excess cleaner before inserting it into your dog's ears. With your fingers, wipe around the opening of the ear canal and as far inside as you can reach without hurting your dog. As long as you are gentle, you will not damage your dog's ear. Never use a cotton swab. If you are not careful or if your dog shakes his head, the cotton swab can penetrate your dog's eardrum or cause serious injury. A Papillon's ear is too small for your finger to be able to reach any important structures, so use only your fingers and a cotton ball. Your dog may shake his head or rub his ears on you or your furniture, so try to wipe any excess cleaner off with a dry cotton ball after cleaning both ears.

Some Papillons may develop tearstains beneath their eyes. This is common in the breed and does not pose any significant health risk. However, yeast can begin to grow in the damp fur, turning the hair red and creating an unpleasant odor. This area can be difficult to clean during baths because you don't want to get shampoo in your dog's eyes, but there are many different wipes and solutions that are safe for use around the eyes. Simply take a wipe or a cotton ball soaked in the solution and squeeze out the excess product. Gently wipe the area beneath your Papillon's eyes, avoiding the eyes if possible. There are also various nutritional supplements on the market claiming to fix tearstains, but most Papillon owners have found mixed results with these products. It may work with some dogs, but unfortunately not all.

When Professional Help is Necessary

You don't always need to be in a difficult situation to ask for help from a professional. Many Papillon owners simply don't have the time or don't have the desire to groom their dogs themselves. This does not make you a bad owner. In fact, it can be helpful with socialization and training to take your dog to the groomer on a regular basis. This accustoms your dog to being handled by strangers and spending time away from home. Groomers are also experts in the health of the dog's skin and coat, so they are able to spot any potential problems that can be treated as soon as possible.

Groomers also know how to handle difficult dogs with a gentle hand, so if you are struggling with grooming, it's best to ask for help sooner than later. Many groomers welcome difficult dogs because they know that after a few grooms, once dogs get to know them, they are usually much easier to handle. Dogs may be nervous about going to the groomer at first, but once they develop a relationship with their new friend, they are often excited to go in for their routine spa day.

CHAPTER 16
Basic Health Care

Visiting the Vet

Routine veterinary appointments are essential to your dog's health. Most vets recommend an exam every 6-12 months, depending on the age and health of your Papillon. It may seem unnecessary to take your dog to the vet this frequently when he or she is not showing any symptoms of health problems, but it's important to be able to catch any conditions before they become serious. Your dog will also need regular vaccinations and deworming. The vet will also be able to give you feedback on your dog's weight and overall health and can make suggestions on any changes that may be needed.

Fleas and Ticks

Fleas and ticks can carry and transmit a variety of diseases to your dogs. If carried into the house, they may also bite and infect you or your family members. Fleas are known to carry tapeworms and bartonellosis and can cause anemia. They can also cause flea allergy dermatitis, which is severe itchiness and skin inflammation due to a reaction to the flea's saliva by your dog's immune system. Ticks can carry Lyme disease, Rocky Mountain spotted fever, ehrlichiosis, and babesiosis. Most tick-borne diseases can be transferred to humans. Flea and tick prevention is essential in keeping your Papillon and your family safe from disease.

Depending on where you live, you may or may not need year-round flea and tick prevention. Some climates allow fleas and ticks to thrive more, so your pet may be more at risk in certain areas of the country. Your veterinarian will be able to advise you on how frequently you need to treat your dog. Some boarding facilities also require dogs to have received flea and tick treatment before staying with them, so if you board your dog often you may want to consider regular treatment. Some areas may experience flea and tick problems all year, while it's only a concern in the summer in other areas.

Your veterinarian will be able to advise you on the best product for the fleas and ticks commonly found in your area. Most flea and tick pre-

138

vention products are packaged in a plastic vial. To apply, simply break the end off the vial and apply the solution to the back of your dog's neck. Since Papillon have such long hair, you may need to part the hair to apply the product directly to the skin. This process will need to be repeated every month or as needed.

Flea and tick collars are another option, but use caution, especially if you have other pets. Some types of flea collar use certain insecticides, such as tetrachlorvinphos, that can cause serious reactions, especially with cats. Some dogs may also experience a negative reaction to flea collars. Symptoms can range from skin irritation and hair loss to gastro-intestinal distress and seizures. Tetrachlorvinphos is also considered a carcinogen by the Environmental Protection Agency and may put you and your human family members at risk, especially if you have children.

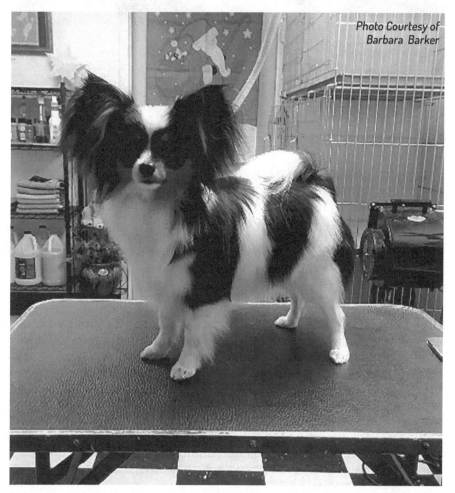

Photo Courtesy of Barbara Barker

Photo Courtesy of Rebecca Johnson

Worms and Parasites

In addition to external parasites, regular veterinary care can prevent and treat internal parasites before they cause serious health problems. The parasites most frequently found in dogs will depend on the area you live in, but your local veterinarian will be equipped to detect and treat any parasite. Many intestinal parasites can also be passed on to humans, so keeping your dog parasite free is essential to preventing the infection from spreading to your human family members.

Intestinal worms are the most common parasite found in dogs. They are especially common in puppies, who often pick them up from adult dogs in the home. They are usually passed from host to host when an animal ingests the eggs or larvae from contaminated water, soil, food, or another animal's feces. Roundworms, hookworms, whipworms, and tapeworms are the most common type of intestinal worms in dogs. Protozoa such as giardia and coccidia are also common. Heartworms are also frequently found in certain areas and are passed from host to host through mosquitos. A mosquito drinks the infected blood of one animal and passes the parasite onto the next animal it feeds on. Heartworms, as the name implies, live in the heart and can lead to death if the infection is not treated as soon as possible. Heartworm is much more difficult to treat than other common internal parasites. Treatment takes several months to complete, and the dog's activity level must be extremely limited to prevent the worms from blocking arteries, a potentially deadly situation. Luckily, heartworm infections can be prevented with a monthly chewable tablet.

Symptoms of a parasitic infection include vomiting, diarrhea, anemia, and weight loss. Dogs with a particularly heavy parasite load may appear to have a distended stomach with an otherwise malnourished body. Infected dogs may be lethargic or may exhibit a severe cough. Some dogs may exhibit no symptoms at all.

Your veterinarian will be able to detect intestinal parasites through a fecal exam. A small sample of your dog's feces is examined under a microscope in search of eggs or larvae. Determining the type of worm infecting the dog is crucial in prescribing the correct treatment. Heartworms can be detected through a simple blood test. A sample of blood is taken from your dog and mixed with a chemical solution and placed into a testing device. After about fifteen minutes, the results will be ready to read. Depending on the type of parasite detected, your dog will receive either oral medication or injections. Treatment time will vary from just a few days to several months. Regular testing is key in preventing any parasite from causing permanent damage to your dog's health.

Holistic Alternatives and Supplements

Photo Courtesy of Morgan Fitzgerald

If you prefer a more natural way of living, you may consider finding a holistic veterinarian in your area. Holistic veterinary medicine involves treating the animal with an appropriate combination of both conventional and alternative therapies. Patients may be treated with the same modern medications and surgeries that you would find in more conventional veterinary practices. However, those therapies may be combined with treatments such as acupuncture, chiropractic adjustments, herbal medicine, and nutritional therapy.

Holistic care can be especially helpful with chronic conditions, or those that have been difficult to treat using conventional veterinary medicine. This is not to say that there is no use for conventional Western medicine. On the contrary, in emergency situations where surgery is needed, conventional treatment may be necessary to save the animal's life. However, if a pet is suffering from a chronic illness such as kidney disease, holistic medicine may offer a different solution to the problem.

Holistic medicine treats the body as a whole rather than individual parts. For example, if your Papillon suffers from arthritis in his back, a holistic veterinarian may try a combination of nutritional supplements, acupuncture, or massage. Even though the problem is mainly in the dog's back, the vet will focus on improving the dog's overall health and well-being in an effort to help the specific problem.

If you'd like to consult a holistic veterinary medicine, the American Holistic Veterinary Medical Association has a list of approved holistic veterinarians on their website in both the United States and Canada. The site allows you to search by the species treated by the vet, as well as the specific treatments offered. Many vets specialize in certain species or therapies and the website helps owners narrow down the options to suit their individual needs.

Vaccinations

All dogs will require vaccinations for common diseases, such as rabies and parvovirus. These vaccines are referred to as core vaccines, because they are recommended no matter where you live. Depending on your area, your Papillon may also receive non-core vaccines, such as leptospirosis and kennel cough.

Core vaccines are often given in combination, with antibodies for several diseases contained in one syringe. The most common vaccine is called a five-way, or DHPP, and protects against parvovirus, distemper, adenovirus cough, hepatitis, and parainfluenza. Your vet may also offer a seven-way vaccine that also protects against leptospirosis and coronavirus. Core vaccines are initially given in a series of three, normally at six, twelve, and sixteen weeks of age. Thereafter, they are given once yearly or once every three years, depending on your vet and the area you live in.

The only core vaccine required by law is the rabies vaccine. Rabies vaccines are typically first given at around 16 weeks of age. After the first vaccine, the second is typically given after one year. As the dog reaches adulthood, rabies vaccines may be given yearly or once every three years, depending on your vet's recommendation. Some areas require dogs by law to be vaccinated yearly.

Examples of common non-core vaccines include leptospirosis, Lyme disease, kennel cough, and rattlesnake venom. Non-core vaccines may or may not be recommended by your vet. Typically, they do not protect the animal for as long as the core vaccines and they may not be as effective, depending on the specific strains of the diseases in your area. Many boarding kennels require dogs to have received a recent kennel cough or bordatella vaccine, so if you plan on boarding your dog, you may need to make an appointment with your veterinarian first. Discuss non-core vaccines with your vet to decide whether they are appropriate for your Papillon.

Allergic reactions to vaccines are not uncommon, especially in small dogs. Vaccines only come in one size, so a Papillon will receive the same vaccine as a Great Dane. Most Papillon owners and breeders recommend giving only one vaccine at a time. If your dog is due for both five-way and rabies vaccines, ask your vet to give only one and make an appointment for a later time for the other. Signs of an allergic reaction include lethargy, swelling of the face or paws, hives, vomiting, and pain or swelling around the injection site. More severe reactions may include difficulty breathing and seizures. If your dog shows any reaction after receiving

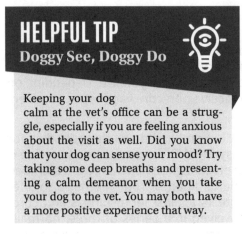

HELPFUL TIP
Doggy See, Doggy Do

Keeping your dog calm at the vet's office can be a struggle, especially if you are feeling anxious about the visit as well. Did you know that your dog can sense your mood? Try taking some deep breaths and presenting a calm demeanor when you take your dog to the vet. You may both have a more positive experience that way.

a vaccine, take him or her back to the vet immediately. Serious reactions can be life-threatening if not treated quickly.

Some veterinarians offer titer testing as an alternative to yearly vaccines. Titer testing measures the antibodies in your Papillon's blood and if their levels are high enough, they are not required to be vaccinated. Titer testing is only recommended for core vaccines, as non-core vaccines typically are not long-lasting enough to have the appropriate levels of antibodies for any significant period of time. Your vet will draw a small sample of blood and will either test the blood in-house or send it off to a lab for testing. If the antibody levels are low, your pet likely is not protected against the disease and will need to be vaccinated. Titer testing can be more expensive than yearly vaccines, but if your dog is prone to serious reactions, it may be a better option to ensure he has the protection he needs without risking his health more often than necessary.

Pet Insurance

Although typically not as expensive as human health care, the cost for veterinary care can be quite high, especially with emergencies. Pet insurance is rising in popularity as veterinary care costs reach new heights, and many Papillon owners have chosen to purchase pet insurance to protect their pet and their wallet. There are many companies that offer a variety of plans for different budgets. You can choose your plan based on the amount of coverage and the cost of the monthly premium. As with your own health insurance, some pets may cost more to insure or may be denied coverage due to preexisting conditions.

Unlike human health insurance, pet insurance usually does not help cover the cost of routine care. Your regular exams and vaccinations will probably need to be paid for out of pocket. A few companies do offer plans to cover routine care, but they can be expensive. However, if your Papillon is hit by a car or is diagnosed with cancer, pet insurance can help cover the cost of treatment.

Papillon owners are divided on whether pet insurance is worth the cost. Those who have had pet insurance cover the cost of major surgeries or treatments are avid supporters, but others have healthy pets who have remained accident free for many years and those monthly premiums do add up. Many owners would rather put that same amount of money away every month into an emergency savings account for use in the event of an accident or illness. Do your research with several different companies to determine whether pet insurance is right for your individual situation, or whether it would be better to save your money.

CHAPTER 17
Advanced Papillon Health and Aging Dog Care

Common Diseases and Conditions in Papillons

"As with all toy breeds luxating patellas can be an issue. The breed CHIC (Parent Club recommended health tests) is for Patellas, hearts, and eyes. The eyes are checked by a veterinary ophthalmologist and CERFed (certified) free of eye disease. This test must be reCERFed every couple of years. Cataracts and Progressive Retinal Atrophy (PRA) can be seen in Papillons. There is a genetic test for PRA1 and most reputable breeders have tested their breeding stock. The parent club has done a good job as the incidence of eye disease is low."

Elyse Vandermolen
Clearlake Papillons

Although Papillons are generally considered to be a healthy breed, there are a few conditions that commonly affect the breed. Allergies are a growing concern among dogs of all breeds. Dogs of any age can develop sensitivities to certain proteins in their food or allergens in their environment. Small breeds, such as Papillons, are also prone to dental disease. Tartar and plaque can build up quickly, causing gum inflammation and painful abscesses. Luckily, all these conditions are treatable and can be managed with regular veterinary care.

Just as with humans, Papillons can develop allergies to a wide variety of substances. Allergic reactions are the result of the body's immune system responding to a certain protein that has been introduced into the body through food, the airway, or physical contact. Dogs usually don't develop allergies until after at least six months of age, with most dogs being diagnosed after one or two years of age. One of the first indicators of an allergy is the dog experiencing itchiness in general or itchiness in a specific area of the body. He may also cough, sneeze, or wheeze, or have runny discharge from the nose or eyes. If the allergy affects the digestive tract, as in a food allergy, the dog may experience vomiting or diarrhea. The allergen caus-ing the problem will need to be identified in order to treat the problem. If the dog is allergic to chicken, it would be better to re-move chicken from the diet rath-er than use medication to con-trol the symptoms. Dogs with sensitivities to common proteins in dog food such as beef, chick-en, or lamb, may have more suc-cess with foods containing nov-el proteins such as salmon, pork, or kangaroo.

Photo Courtesy of Ken Rosenbaum

Prescription diets are also available to dogs with more severe food allergies. If the dog is allergic to a protein he comes into contact with such as grasses, pesticides, or certain materials, avoidance of those pro-teins would be recommended if possible. Some dogs may also develop allergies to certain pollens or airborne proteins. If the removal of the al-lergens from the dog's environment is not possible, there are a wide va-riety of medications available to control the symptoms. Be aware that most allergy medications suppress the immune system in one way or another and may cause side effects. Discuss all treatment and medica-tion in depth with your veterinarian when deciding how to treat your Pa-pillon's allergies.

Periodontal disease is also common in Papillons and other small breeds. Small dogs are more prone to dental problems than larger breeds, due in part to their small mouth size. Toy breeds have the same number of teeth as any other breed of dog, but those teeth are typical-ly crowded into a much smaller mouth. It's also more common for small dogs to be fed a diet of canned food, or a homemade diet. There can be many factors contributing to periodontal disease in Papillons, but it's es-sential to keep an eye on the health of your dog's teeth throughout his life. If you notice your dog is reluctant to eat or that there is a foul odor coming from the dog's mouth, it may be time to speak to a vet. Some owners opt to have a yearly dental cleaning performed on their dogs as part of their health-care routine. Once per year is often enough for healthy dogs with few dental problems, but if your dog has a history of poor dental health, he may need to see the vet every six months or so. Without treatment, periodontal disease can lead to painful abscesses and tooth loss. The bacteria present in tartar can enter the bloodstream and infect vital organs. Thankfully, periodontal disease is completely pre-ventable with regular dental care and veterinary exams.

Genetic Traits Found in Papillons

There are a few genetic problems that are common in Papillons, but most reputable breeders are working hard to eliminate these conditions from the breed's gene pool. Papillons are also prone to a common heart problem known as mitral valve disease. The Orthopedic Foundation for Animals recommends that Papillons undergo testing for all of these conditions before being bred to prevent any genetic problems from being passed down to future generations.

Papillons are not exempt from one of the most common orthopedic problems in small dogs. According to Elyse Vandermolen of Clearlake Papillons, "As with all toy breeds, luxating patellas can be an issue." Patellar luxation is when a dog's kneecap slips out of its normal position within its groove in the femur bone. A normal patella, or kneecap, stays within this groove reliably during all stages of movement of the hind leg. A luxating patella, however, will slip out of the groove and to the side at certain points in the movement of the leg. Severe luxating patellas may not be able to stay within the groove at all and may only be placed back into the groove with physical manipulation.

Dogs with luxating patellas may appear to skip occasionally while walking or running. This hopping motion is often enough to slide the patella back into place in the lower grades of the disorder. As the dog ages, the condition may get worse and it may become more difficult for the patella to stay in place. Luxating patellas at any grade can be fixed surgically. The surgeon simple deepens the groove, making it more difficult for the patella to slide out. It can be a long recovery, and physical activity must be limited for several weeks, but owners almost always see an improvement in their dog's mobility post-surgery. This condition is genetic, so Papillons who have been diagnosed with luxating patellas should not be bred.

Cataracts are a disease of the eye lens, typically brought on by age, trauma, or certain health conditions such as diabetes or nutritional deficiencies. Most cataracts have a cloudy, blue-gray appearance, but may or may not cause vision problems. If the cataract is quite small, the dog may still be able to see quite well. If left untreated, cataracts can progress and lead to a complete loss of vision. Fortunately, cataracts are treatable and the outcome is usually positive if the disease is caught in its early stages. Depending on the severity of the condition and the age of the dogs, treatment may consist of oral supplements, eye drops, or even surgery. Catching the disease early is key to preventing permanent damage to the eye, so regular veterinary examinations are necessary, especially if your dog has a family history of eye problems.

Progressive retinal atrophy, or PRA, is a degenerative eye disease affecting adult Papillons. The condition, which is a progressive degeneration of the dog's eye structure, typically worsens with age. For some dogs, it may take several years before any noticeable loss of vision is noted, but others may completely lose their sight in just a few months or even weeks. PRA first destroys the rods of the eye, which are responsible for sight in low-light environments, so owners typically notice their dogs struggling to see in dimly lit rooms or at night. As the disease advances, the loss of sight will progress to all light levels, eventually leading to complete blindness. The disease is not curable, but the degeneration can be slowed with a daily regimen of certain antioxidants.

The most common heart disease affecting Papillons is mitral valve disease. Mitral valve disease is caused by the weakening of the mitral valve in the heart. Over time, the valve becomes deformed and does not shut as tightly as it should. Blood then leaks back through the opening and puts excess strain on the heart. The disease is more commonly diagnosed in older Papillons, but younger dogs may also be affected. Symptoms of heart disease are lethargy, coughing, labored breathing, and an elevated heart and respiratory rate. Unfortunately, there is no cure for heart disease, but it can be treated. With proper care and medication, dogs may live for several years after diagnosis. Again, the sooner the disease can be caught, the more effective treatment will be.

Photo Courtesy of
Danielle Grenier

Illness and Injury Prevention

Although not every illness or injury can be prevented, properly managing your dog's lifestyle and healthcare routine can help your dog avoid any serious health problems. Regular checkups with your veterinarian are essential in preventing illness and catching any problems in their early stages. The sooner a problem is detected, the sooner it can be treated. You must also manage your dog while at home and on the go. Papillons are small, delicate dogs with big personalities, so care must be taken to keep them out of harm's way. Most Papillons will gladly get into trouble if given the opportunity. Larger playmates, long flights of stairs, and open doors are all potential disasters, so you must always keep an eye out for any potential dangers.

Basics of Senior Dog Care

Small breeds are typically considered to be senior, or geriatric, at around eight years of age. This does not mean you need to change your dog's lifestyle on his eighth birthday. Certain health conditions may slow your dog down earlier and he may exhibit the signs of old age before he turns eight. Likewise, a fit and healthy dog may not act like a senior until much later in life. Small dogs, such as Papillons, usually live around 12-17 years, so the age at which you notice them slowing down may vary.

As your Papillon ages you may notice changes in his body and behavior. You may notice your dog sleeping more and getting tired more quickly on walks. He may seem stiff getting out of his bed in the morning. If his hearing or sight is deteriorating, he may become more cautious on walks and respond less to your calls. As aging dogs lose their sense of sight and hearing, you may need to be more cautious when waking your dog from naps or approaching them from behind. Older dogs typically gain more weight, though some have a difficult time keeping weight on and may become quite thin. You may also notice your senior Papillon needing to go outside more often or having accidents in the house. Incontinence is a common problem in older dogs. Some dogs may also develop symptoms of cognitive dysfunction, or dementia, and may act differently or seem confused at times. It's essential to notice these signs of aging and adapt your dog's care accordingly.

Photo Courtesy of
Natalie Iezzi

Grooming

As your Papillon ages, his grooming needs may change too. It's important for senior dogs to continue to be groomed on a regular basis. This time together gives you or your groomer the opportunity to check the overall quality of your dog's skin and coat. Some aging dogs may experience thinning hair or develop lumps and bumps. Grooming gives you the chance to put your hands on the dog in a more thorough way than you would with regular affection.

Senior Papillons may need their groomer to be more patient as they become more affected by the conditions of old age. Standing for long periods of time may become more difficult. Many groomers work with senior dogs in different sessions, allowing them to rest for a few minutes before moving on to the next step in the grooming process. Some dogs may also begin to develop symptoms of dementia and they may become more difficult to work with. They may exhibit signs of fear or aggression, even if they were well-behaved for the groomer in their youth. Groomers will need to be especially cautious brushing older dogs because of tender joints and delicate skin.

Nutrition

Aging Papillons will also need their diet to be adapted to the changes in their bodies. As their metabolism slows, their caloric needs decrease, so many senior dog food formulas are lower in calories than regular adult dog food. Obesity in senior dogs is a common problem, and care must be taken to avoid excess weight. An overweight dog puts more strain on its aging, arthritic joints, which can lead to pain and a further decrease in mobility. Some older dogs may lose weight quickly. This can be due to a loss of appetite or a health condition, so if you notice any sudden changes in your dog's weight you should speak with your veterinarian.

Older pets may also develop certain health conditions that require a change in diet. Diabetic dogs, or those suffering from liver or heart disease, will need special food, sometimes requiring a prescription from your veterinarian. Older dogs may also need more fiber in their diet to help ease any gastrointestinal difficulties brought on by age.

You may also consider adding supplements to your senior Papillon's diet. Joint supplements such as glucosamine and chondroitin sulfate can ease joint pain. Adding a fiber supplement or probiotics will help older dogs who suffer from digestive issues. Older dogs that have lost their appetite may also need appealing additions to their meals such as bone broth, warm water, or canned food. Before adding any supplements to your Papillon's diet, discuss your dog's problems with your vet to rule out any underlying serious health conditions.

Exercise

A slowing metabolism and aching joints can cause even the most rambunctious Papillon to slow down as it ages. Even the healthiest of dogs slow down as they age, but the exact age at which this occurs can vary. Certain conditions may also limit your dog's mobility earlier in life. Care must be taken to manage a senior dog's weight. Obesity can strain aging joints and discourage older dogs from exercising as much as they should, leading to further weight gain. However, dogs should not be forced to exercise too much as this can also have damaging effects on joints.

No matter what age your Papillon's mobility begins to decrease, you must provide a safe and healthy environment for your dog to exercise in. Slick floors or long flights of stairs can spell trouble for senior dogs, so rather than an indoor game of fetch, try taking your dog outside for a brief walk through the grass. As your senior dog's energy levels decrease,

Photo Courtesy of
Candace Brunskole

Photo Courtesy of Jordan Stephens

you may consider offering more mental stimulation and less physical stimulation. Many older dogs' bodies slow down well before their minds, and mental stimulation, such as puzzles or scent work, can be a great way to keep them busy without causing discomfort.

Common Old-Age Ailments

As Papillons age, they will likely develop arthritis in different parts of their body and they may lose their sight or hearing. They may sleep most of the day and only want to go for short walks. Some dogs may become confused or startle more easily. As your Papillon gets older, it's important to make the necessary changes in your lifestyle or schedule to accommodate his changing needs. He may need to go outside more often or may need a change in diet. Some dogs can become more difficult to manage in their older years, but it's important to remember the years of joy you've shared and treasure these final years together.

When It's Time to Say Goodbye

Saying goodbye to your beloved Papillon won't be easy, but this is not a time for only mourning. Reflect on your dog's life and all the joy he has given you over the years. Be thankful for your time together and remember the good times.

As the end nears, it can be difficult to make the necessary arrangements, but veterinary professionals will be there to help you through it. Many veterinarians offer both in-office and in-home euthanasia services. For some dogs and owners, it can be difficult to say goodbye in the sterile environment of an exam room. For others, they would rather not have the memory of the end in their home. Whichever you would prefer, you will be able to find a comforting and supportive veterinary team to help you through this difficult time. The most important aspect of saying goodbye is being there with your devoted Papillon. He will find comfort in knowing his last moments were spent with the person or people he loves the most.

> **HELPFUL TIP**
> **Remembering**
>
> Papillons are excellent companion dogs, so when it's time to say goodbye, it may feel like parting with a best friend. Many services are now available to help dog owners cherish the memory of their pets. Artisans can be found on online marketplaces such as Etsy and offer memorials from hand-painted portraits, to custom grave markers, to commemorative key chains, so that the memory of your beloved pet is never far from your heart.

Your veterinarian will likely have several options for your dog's remains. If you would prefer not to deal with the remains yourself, your veterinary team will be happy to take care of the disposal in a dignified and respectful manner. Many vets also offer cremation services. If you choose to do so, the ashes can be returned to you after the cremation. Some clinics offer a variety of urns or you can choose a simple box. Many owners choose to discuss these options with their vet ahead of time, so they have a plan when the time comes.

Creating a memorial can help you to treasure the memories of your beloved family member and help you through the grieving process. Owners often choose to memorialize their Papillons with personalized stones, tiles, or garden decorations. Others choose jewelry made from their dog's nose or paw prints. There are even companies that will create a necklace from your beloved pet's ashes. However you choose to remember your Papillon, cherish the memories and remember the unconditional love you were given.

Made in United States
Troutdale, OR
02/20/2025

29125882R00086